P9-DBT-922

GREAT DISCOVERIES IN SCIENCE

The Theory of Relativity

by Lisa Hiton

Cavendish
Square

New York

Published in 2017 by Cavendish Square Publishing, LLC
243 5th Avenue, Suite 136, New York, NY 10016

Copyright © 2017 by Cavendish Square Publishing, LLC

First Edition

No part of this publication may be reproduced, stored in a retrieval system, or transmitted in any form or by any means—electronic, mechanical, photocopying, recording, or otherwise—without the prior permission of the copyright owner. Request for permission should be addressed to Permissions, Cavendish Square Publishing, 243 5th Avenue, Suite 136, New York, NY 10016. Tel (877) 980-4450; fax (877) 980-4454.

Website: cavendishsq.com

This publication represents the opinions and views of the author based on his or her personal experience, knowledge, and research. The information in this book serves as a general guide only. The author and publisher have used their best efforts in preparing this book and disclaim liability rising directly or indirectly from the use and application of this book.

CPSIA Compliance Information: Batch #CS16CSQ

All websites were available and accurate when this book was sent to press.

Library of Congress Cataloging-in-Publication Data

Names: Hiton, Lisa, author.
Title: The theory of relativity / Lisa Hiton.
Description: New York : Cavendish Square Publishing, [2016] | Series:
Great discoveries in science | Includes bibliographical references and
index. | Description based on print version record and CIP data provided
by publisher; resource not viewed.
Identifiers: LCCN 2016001225 (print) | LCCN 2015051007 (ebook) | ISBN
9781502619488 (ebook) | ISBN 9781502619471 (library bound)
Subjects: LCSH: Relativity (Physics) | Quantum theory.
Classification: LCC QC173.55 (print) | LCC QC173.55 .H58 2016 (ebook) | DDC
530.11--dc23
LC record available at http://lccn.loc.gov/2016001225

Editorial Director: David McNamara
Editor: Caitlyn Paley
Copy Editor: Michele Suchomel-Casey
Art Director: Jeffrey Talbot
Designer: Joseph Macri
Senior Production Manager: Jennifer Ryder-Talbot
Photo Research: J8 Media

The photographs in this book are used by permission and through the courtesy of: Mark Garlic/Science Photo Library/Getty Images, cover; Jack Turner/Library of Congress/File:Albert Einstein 1947.jpg/Wikimedia Commons, 4; Science Source, 8; Ted Kinsman/Science Source, 11; Peter Fitzgerald/File:Metra map.svg/Wikimedia Commons, 16; Universal Images Group/Getty Images, 18; Laguna Design/Science Photo Library/Getty Images, 26; Pasieka/Science Photo Library/Getty Images, 30; John Rensten/Getty Images, 31; Source:Albert Einstein, Relativity: The Special and General Theory, 36; Encyclopaedia Britannica/UIG/Universal Images Group/Getty Images, 39; Source:Albert Einstein, Relativity: The Special and General Theory, 41; Hulton Archive/Getty Images, 46; http://www.sil.si.edu/digitalcollections/hst/scientific-identity/CF/display_results.cfm?alpha_sort=p /File:Max Planck (1858-1947).jpg/Wikimedia Commons, 48; Encyclopaedia Britannica/UIG Via Getty Images, 50; Emilio Segrè Visual Archives/American Institute of Physics/Science Source, 53; Macauley, Charles Raymond, 1871-1934/ U.S. Library of Congress http://www.loc.gov/pictures/item/acd1996005205/PP/File:Einstein-cartoon1.jpg/Wikimedia Commons, 59; Science Source, 60; NASA, 62; Source:Albert Einstein, Relativity: The Special and General Theory, 69; Mdd4696 at English Wikipedia/Transferred from en.wikipedia (http://en.wikipedia.org) to Commons by Hansmuller/File:Time-dilation-002.svg/Wikimedia Commons, 71; Laguna Design/Science Source, 79; Stib at en.wikipedia (http://en.wikipedia.org)/ Transferred from en.wikipedia (http://en.wikipedia.org)/(Original text : self-made)/File:World line.svg/Wikimedia Commons, 80; KSmrq/Own work, self-made using gnuplot with manual alterations/File:Relativistic precession.svg/Wikimedia Commons, 82; NASA, ESA, and the Hubble SM4 ERO Team via Getty Images, 86; Paul Wootton/Science Source, 89; X-ray: NASA/CXC/Rutgers/J.Hughes; Optical: NASA/STScI/ http://astropix.ipac.caltech.edu/image/chandra/587b [direct link (http://images.ipac.caltech.edu/chandra/587b/chandra_587b_3600.jpg)]; see alsohttp://chandra.harvard.edu/photo/2015/iyl/ File:NASA-SNR0519690-ChandraX-RayObservatory-20150122.jpg/Wikimedia Commons, 92; Original image by User:Vlad2i, slightly modified by User:mapos/File:Gravitational red-shifting2.png/Wikimedia Commons, 93; User:Alain r/File:BH LMC.png/Wikimedia Commons, 95.

Printed in the United States of America

Contents

Albert Einstein's theories shaped our modern understanding of physics.

Introduction

Among the twentieth century's most important public figures, Albert Einstein made his mark by shaping our understanding of the universe. Einstein looked at the universe as an object with rules and laws that govern it, rules that had not yet been discovered. Einstein's equation $E = mc^2$, developed through many theoretical experiments, is perhaps the most groundbreaking equation in physics to date. The equation says that energy equals mass times the speed of light, squared. $E = mc^2$ is so famous that it's found on T-shirts and posters and is mentioned in popular television shows. Even people who don't know its meaning have heard it. The fame of the equation is well deserved, and the equation is a direct result of Einstein's theory of relativity. This theory of relativity mentions that time and space are woven together. Einstein stated that the speed of light is constant. He stated that gravity is not a universal force, but rather, relative to other massive objects.

Einstein was born in 1879; and this year is relevant to science. The same year that Einstein was born, world-famous physicist James Clerk Maxwell died. Considered the most famous physicist behind Einstein and Isaac Newton, Maxwell's work would be the seed that led Einstein to his many scientific discoveries. Maxwell's work in **electrodynamics** contributed to the world's understanding of light, magnets, sound waves, and the like. These occurrences, which are often unseen by the naked eye, can be quantified because of Maxwell's work. It's also a strange coincidence that he died the year Einstein was born. Newton was born the year that Galileo died. It seems almost fated that these gigantic names should be instantly replaced by the next great scientific thinker.

Einstein's genius would remain unseen until the 1920s. His work, initially, seemed strange to many scientists. He had ideas that were radical. Everything he said—especially his theory of relativity—seemed just a bit counterintuitive to the science that came before him.

But, as time passed, Einstein's ideas about relativity were proven over and over again. During his career, inventions came along that allowed scientists to see inside the atom, test subatomic particles, and even begin to measure them. Einstein's ideas, as well as the world of the atom, helped us see the universe in a new way. While the old world disappeared into the past with the start of the First World War, Einstein's new ideas were at the forefront of changing the world at the dawn of the Second World War. Einstein and his comrades were able to invent the atomic bomb before the Germans, changing the fate of human history.

Einstein's ideas contain paradoxes: while some scientists believed that light was made up of particles, others believed light was made of waves. Einstein came along and insisted that light is made of both. This seems hard to prove and strange, and yet, his simple equation $E = mc^2$ does successfully prove that this paradox is true.

Like his ideas, Einstein was also a complex figure, full of paradoxes. While on the one hand he was a pacifist, war resistor, and eventual refugee, on the other hand, he enticed the US to create nuclear weapons before Germany could beat America to it. Though he was known for his belief that science should understand nature, he was also known as a daydreamer—a mad scientist with his head in the clouds. Some knew him as being aloof and mostly disinterested in others. Other people considered him a man of the world—playing violin with his friends, speaking out against racism, and conducting public debates about science.

His personal life follows this, too. He married more than once. He had multiple children. In some instances he was considered compassionate, in others he was aloof or disinterested.

As Einstein's ideas about relativity continue to be proven right, we've been able to advance science far past early ideas about physics. This book examines Einstein's path to developing the theories of **general relativity** and **special relativity**, his life, and the ways that other scientists laid the foundation of his groundbreaking ideas. Yet Einstein's theories are more than mere ideas—they continue to shape inventions of today and of the future.

In the story of universal gravitation, Newton developed his ideas about physics when observing an apple fall from a tree.

CHAPTER 1

The Problem of Classical Mechanics

From the seventeenth century until the turn of the twentieth century, the findings of one man stood the test of time. Sir Isaac Newton's ideas explained the motion of our everyday encounters, as well as the motion of the planets. Newton could not have imagined the technological advances that would come after his lifetime, though. And as those inventions came into being, scientists were able to observe the world more closely. Some of these inventions and discoveries include the X-ray, radium, television, high-powered telescopes, computers, uranium, and photon accelerators.

As we began to see the behavior of objects smaller and larger than ourselves, scientists realized that matter was not behaving quite as Newton predicted. It would take many scientists, experiments, and ideas to update a century's worth of math and science. Yet by the time Einstein was a young adult, the phenomena that didn't match Newton's descriptions helped him not only see the forest for the trees, but see a new forest altogether: special and general relativity.

Newton's understanding of the world was three-dimensional. His work claimed that **absolute time** and **absolute space** work with a universal force—gravity—upon which all other action occurs. These ideas hold true to our day-to-day lives. We often use his rules as catchphrases. For instance, we say that opposites attract and that for every action there's an equal and opposite reaction. All day long, we see things fall and hit the ground. We see things at rest suddenly go into motion. We understand the orbit of the planets as they happen on Newton's stage.

Truer, still, are Einstein's ideas. We use his ideas casually, too: *it's all relative*. Einstein would come into the world to humble us and change science. In short, Einstein's theories were developed thanks to earlier understandings of physics. They were also developed in opposition to some of these ideas, which were rules too rigid to explain our universe.

GEOMETRY and EARLY COSMOLOGY

A huge shift in human history came during the Renaissance. Among the many movements that advanced the development of Western thought, the Scientific Revolution stands out. The central figure of the Scientific Revolution was an Italian astronomer, physicist, and philosopher: Galileo Galilei.

One of Galileo's largest contributions to science during this time was a heliocentric understanding of the cosmos. He suggested that Earth is round and orbits around the sun. During this time, such claims went vehemently against the beliefs of the Catholic Church. The church held fast to the idea that the cosmos revolved around Earth, an idea inherited from thinkers like Aristotle and Ptolemy that were established in ancient Greece. Galileo's ideas were considered outrageous and radical throughout his life, even leading to his incarceration.

The heliocentric model of the cosmos includes other mathematic and scientific laws that served to expand our understanding of Earth and the cosmos. Heliocentrism shows Galileo's respect for the relationships between the fields in

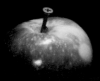

We can observe universal acceleration by dropping two objects of different weights from the same height. The objects will fall at the same speed.

which he worked: math, **astronomy**, experimental physics, and theoretical physics. For example, the idea of a planet's orbit relates to his deep understanding of a parabola. The parabola is a curved line and is relevant to geometry. But in heliocentrism, it relates to more than two dimensions drawn on a plane—it paved the way for many contributions (by Galileo and others to follow) about motion.

Galileo conducted an experiment referred to these days as "falling bodies." Galileo hypothesized that—contrary to Aristotle's claims that heavier objects fall at a greater speed than lighter ones—two objects of different masses would fall at the same speed in a vacuum (the Latin term for "in a vacuum" is *in vacuo*). These days, we can measure the idea pretty easily in a clear tube. If we place two objects of different weights, say a feather and a penny, in the tube and flip it over, the two will hit the bottom at the same time. This revelation is what we call uniform acceleration. This is the basis for understanding Newtonian physics and Einstein's work centuries later.

The idea that an object retains its velocity unless it is interrupted changed the way we relate to time and space. Without having the word and all the equations yet, this idea of velocity begins to account for gravity—a force unknown and unnamed. From this experiment, the whole of **classical mechanics** and **quantum mechanics** was born.

CLASSICAL MECHANICS

In 1687, in a publication called *Philosophiae Naturalis Principia Mathematica*, Sir Isaac Newton provided a study of the motion of bodies. The biggest concern of the field rests in a set of physical laws, laws that validate our reality. These laws by Newton and others were accepted as fact primarily in the eighteenth and nineteenth centuries. The laws and principles mostly describe objects (which we will later call "**reference bodies**") that are tangible and real. Newton's principles about motion came from bodies that are in motion as well as at rest. Our basic equations in physics come from Newton's Laws of Motion:

1. Every body preserves in its state of rest, or of uniform motion in a right line unless it is compelled to change that state by forces impressed thereon. In common speech, we say: A body at rest remains at rest, and a body in motion remains in motion with a constant speed and in a straight line unless acted upon by an outside force.

2. The alteration of motion is ever proportional to the motive force impressed; and is made in the direction of the right line in which that force is impressed. We articulate this today as $F = ma$.

3. To every action, there is always opposed an equal reaction: or the mutual actions of two bodies upon each other are always equal, and directed to contrary parts. To every action, there is an equal and opposite reaction.

As you can see even from the broad overview of these three central laws, classical mechanics deals with physical objects in physical realities. This is a relevant distinction as conceptual thinkers came to develop abstract truths about the universe as history progressed. Newton was fiercely convincing because his laws deal with the here and now of objects. His laws also seem applicable, at least broadly, to the cosmos. By focusing on objects that could be perceived and measured in their motion or stillness, Newton was able to give people the math that backed these ideas. Providing mathematical proof becomes increasingly harder as our understanding of expanse in the universe becomes more abstract. Further, many technological advances will need to happen in order to continue proving physicists correct in their ideas about the world at the atomic level as well as in **cosmology**. We have to think of Newton and classical mechanics as being "common sense," while that which comes later can't always be seen.

A key function of Newton's ideas is that time and space are universal. This is a crucial point to understand the difference between classical mechanics and what we'll learn about relativity later.

Newton's idea of absolute time seems simple: time passes and is perceived identically by all bodies. The time between events is perceived as the same by all observers. Let's say, for example, that a train leaves the city of Chicago at 1:00 p.m. and arrives in Deerfield, Illinois, at 2:04 p.m. The person waiting for the train perceives his wait for the train's arrival identically to the commuter on the train. There are two observers involved in this example, and yet, neither of them impacts how much time passes. Time, in this sense, is constant as is the rate with which it passes, no matter the observer.

To continue with the above example, Newton also accounts for space. In this case, that means the distance that the train travels. From Chicago to Deerfield, the distance between the stops is universal and unchanging. We can see this in geometry, as well as the two points on a grid or map that can be measured. In his seminal work, Newton describes absolute space as:

> Absolute space, in its own nature, without regard to anything external, remains always similar and immovable. Relative space is some movable dimension or measure of the absolute spaces; which our senses determine by its position to bodies: and which is vulgarly taken for immovable space ... Absolute motion is the translation of a body from one absolute

place into another: and relative motion, the translation from one relative place into another …

These ideas seem to match our reality on Earth. As in the example of the train, time and space seem to be consistent and unwavering—they cannot be impacted by any object in motion or an observer, which moves or stays still. Time and space are the stage upon which action happens. In this sense, Newton thought, an observer or body in motion is relative to those two absolute truths. To that end, Newton also gave us the math equations to measure the speed and force of objects in motion.

Velocity, Speed, and the Law of Inertia

Newton's first law gives us inertia. If we were to take a marble and place it on a flat surface, the marble would not move. In this case, the marble and the table need to be in vacuo, or, not impacted by external conditions. For example, if we put the marble on a table outside in the middle of a storm, the weather may impact the table and/or the marble, which could result in a different outcome.

Alternatively, if we place the marble at the top of a ramp, it will speed up and roll down the ramp. If the ramp never ends, the marble will not stop moving either. If we put the marble at the bottom of a ramp and try to roll it upward, the speed of the marble is slower than when it races down to the bottom. Further, there will be a point at which the marble will begin rolling backward down the ramp. This moment of turning and returning toward its start point illuminates Newton's later claims about gravity as a universal force. If the marble is on a level surface and we roll it, the marble will neither speed up nor slow down. Theoretically, in vacuo, it would be able to maintain this speed forever.

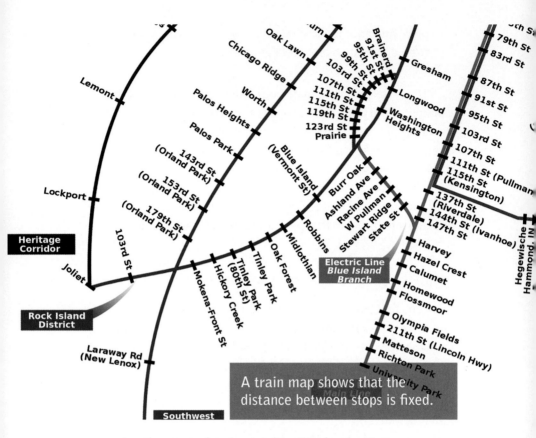

A train map shows that the distance between stops is fixed.

Another part of understanding this first law is to understand the interrupting power of other forces, namely gravity. A famous physics experiment to show this is to take a coin, place it on a piece of paper or cardboard, and set that up over the open side of a cup. Very briskly, pull the cardboard from beneath the coin. The coin will drop to the bottom of the cup and stop. The object is first inert (motionless), then is interrupted (or, "acted upon") by gravity, and then interrupted by a service. It is now inert again.

It's crucial to understand inertia in order to debunk it. Einstein, effectively, is going to come into history and claim that because time and space are *not* absolute, these laws do not hold outside of our particular **gravitational field**.

The *F = ma* Law of Force and Acceleration

In order to understand the acceleration described by Newton, we must first understand velocity. Because Newton was insistent about the existence of absolute time and absolute space, velocities of any given body (in motion or at rest) are additive and subtractive. Again, this sticks with the common-sense ideals in Newton's work. The equation we use to prove this is:

$$v = d/t$$

Velocity equals distance divided by time. The most obvious example of how we still use this equation is driving a car. If a given driver travels 100 miles in 2 hours, the average speed that she drove is:

$$v = (100 \text{ miles})/(2 \text{ hours})$$

and thus, the average speed was 50 mph.

Now that we understand a bit about velocity, we can move on to acceleration. Acceleration is a measure of the rate of change of a body's velocity over time. In this case, acceleration is used to describe an increased magnitude, change in direction, and decrease in magnitude of the given body. Thus, acceleration can be thought of as any given *change* in the velocity of a body. To deepen our understanding of velocity in the math, we can also now claim that a quantity containing more than one element—magnitude and direction—is a vector. The vector is represented by an arrow.

The main equation of Newton's second law is:

$$F = ma$$

whereby force = mass x acceleration

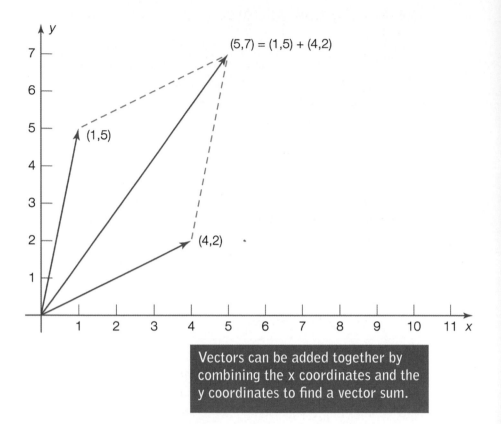

$(5,7) = (1,5) + (4,2)$

(1,5)

(4,2)

Vectors can be added together by combining the x coordinates and the y coordinates to find a vector sum.

Newton is saying that acceleration is produced when a force, or forces, acts on a given mass. For example, an empty freight train car needs less force to be moved from one end of the train tracks to another. On the other hand, once the empty train car is filled with, say, coal, it will need more force to be accelerated back to the other end of the tracks.

Law of Action and Reaction

Newton's third law also demonstrates the elegant simplicity of his absolute truths. For every action, there is an equal and opposite reaction. When you push an object, it pushes back.

This is also expressed as pushing *against* an object and the object pushing back.

This law can be seen in a myriad of everyday experiences. If we go back to the idea of acceleration in the models we've already used, we can see the actions that cause reactions (in this case, accelerations). Turning the ignition in a car is the action, and exhaust is released through an exhaust pipe; the car moves in the opposite direction of its exhaust, which is the reaction. The same is true of the train.

To put it in our hands, let's think of lifting a box. When we lift a box, we feel the weight of the box on our hands and arms. The force of lifting and the force of the box are *absolutely equal* while the direction of force is *opposite*.

$$Fab = -Fab$$

Force is the mutually shared interaction between two bodies.

From these three laws, we understand the way bodies interact with each other. When we expand out from our tangible realities, we see that these laws hold true. In order to continue with proofs, Newton had to give us an understanding of the symmetry of forces. Besides absolute time and absolute space, there is one more absolute phenomenon: gravity. Everything accelerates toward the earth. When a body is thrown up into the air, it comes back down to the ground to return to a state of inertia. But what of the planets and stars, which never become grounded, but rather, go around and around and around?

NEWTON and UNIVERSAL GRAVITY

Based on Newton's understanding of force, more can be concluded when moving away from everyday experience and into the broader universe. Since his laws conclude that force is the shared interaction between bodies, it means that force is a larger phenomenon—part of the stage—like absolute time and absolute space. To this end, Newton claims that the larger central force by which all other bodies abide is gravity. In *Principia*, he describes this universal law of gravitation as such:

> Every massive particle attracts every other massive particle with a force directly proportional to the product of their masses and inversely proportional to the square of distance between them ...

In order for his laws of motion to hold, he expands them out to the cosmos where **universal gravitation** explains *and predicts* the motions of the planets. This in turn also goes to explain the elements themselves—our tides, seasons, etc.

Einstein will later explicate the truth and problems of gravity as universal. For Newton, the role of gravity offers the invisible force of attraction between bodies—the invisible string that holds planets, moons, stars, and suns in what he perceives to be consistent *distance* over given amounts of time. For Newton, this explains the elliptical orbits of planets. It suggests that the sun's **gravitational mass** is greater than that of other planets. Further, the math behind the ever-potent gravity proves that an object's gravitational mass is identical to its **inertial mass**.

Newton's rigid, physical laws explain the universe mechanically. The rules seem and read as common sense. They match our perception of day-to-day experiences on Earth, as well as Earth in relation to what we can observe in the sky. By understanding bodies as having universal gravity, he proves that Earth moves around the sun like clockwork—as in, the

The Legend of Newton's Falling Apple

How is it that Newton came to his revolutionary ideas? Similar to Einstein's thought experiments based on observations, Newton's ideas are said to have come from watching an apple fall from a tree. Newton claimed that seeing the apple fall allowed him to articulate his intuited ideas about gravity. In some versions of this myth, the apple hits Newton on the head. To this day, there are disagreements as to whether or not his theory of gravity arrived to Newton in an instant. Nowadays, it seems that scientists don't believe the apple hit him on the head, but many still argue about how closely his ideas coincided with watching an apple fall.

There are some manuscripts of the account from the 1700s with passages written by Newton's peers that confirm the myth. The second-hand accounts consistently describe Newton wandering around his gardens and seeing the apple fall from the tree straight to the ground. *Why is it the apple always falls straight to the ground? Why not sideways? Why not upward?* It is this image of Newton that is most often recounted.

It is human nature to mythologize, especially when it comes to prodigies. We think of these figures achieving their ideas alone. But it's rare that a discovery is made independently. Even in the case of Newton, the science and geometry he knew before the apple influenced his ability to prove his ideas logically and mathematically. If Newton and his contemporaries hadn't yet believed Earth was round, Newton wouldn't have been able to conceive of gravity in the terms we know it by today.

time it takes to orbit the sun is as predictable as the absolute time such distance occupies.

Newton's universal law of gravitation seemed to be proven true in 1758 when a comet returned to the visible night sky. We know the comet today as Halley's comet, named after the astronomer Edmond Halley, who had seen it and tracked it in instances prior. The math behind Newton's ideas predicts such cosmological observations. These ideas, even with small instances of disbelief, prevailed for many years to come, until Einstein came along and suggested this common sense doesn't quite explain our very complex, infinite, and changing existence, let alone the universe's.

OPTICS and ELECTRODYNAMICS

One of the problems with classical mechanics is the translation of the principles and laws into the theoretical realm of the universe. As technological advances take place, it becomes harder to hold steadfast to these classical laws as, well, law. Optics and electrodynamics became increasingly focused fields of study because of technological advancement and invention, which allow the study of what was once abstract or magical to be tangible and pragmatic.

Considering Newton's views of gravity—that it is the invisible string by which bodies in motion or at rest keep constant distance and time in relation to each other—time and invention bring physicists into more abstract conundrums. For example, how are things like light and sound impacted by gravity? And if they aren't, what does this mean for the ideals we've inherited from Newton?

Austrian physicist Christian Doppler made one particular discovery that pointed the field in the direction of such questions. Like most scientific observations, the **Doppler effect** is first seen in an everyday occurrence, which was then proven by its application to larger universal phenomena. Doppler realized that the use of a siren is perceived with varying frequencies based on where the siren is relative to the observer. When, for example, an ambulance is approaching an observer, the frequency of the siren seems to be higher, whereas, when the ambulance passes the observer, the frequency seems less and less. This observation suggests that upon approach, each emitted sound wave takes less and less time to reach the observer as/because the distance between the observer and the ambulance gets smaller. Although each wave is released in equal succession, the perception is a higher frequency. This is one seed of an idea that Einstein took in order to disprove Newton's understanding of absolute time and absolute space.

The BEGINNINGS of QUANTUM THEORY

From Newton and the field of classical mechanics, we derived rules for a common-sense world—one that matches our human experience. Simultaneously, other physicists sought to understand the less human and more abstract phenomena of the universe. While Newton and his comrades believed they'd generated ideas about the world and the cosmos, other physicists were left wondering about matter in its baser forms: atomic and subatomic particles. We began seeing the validity of these fields through optics and electrodynamics first. These ideas, math equations, and subsequent inventions also inspired an entirely new philosophical field of mechanics: quantum mechanics.

As scientists gained the ability to better understand the micro truths of matter, the limitations of Newton's principles became more obvious. It was at this moment during the twentieth century when the paradigm shifted from classical mechanics and its subfields to quantum mechanics and relativity. In this sense, quantum mechanics and relativity served to truly replace what came before.

Unlike the nineteenth century and what came prior, the rhetoric of the twentieth century dealt with uncertainty. Newton offered a kind of symmetry that mirrored the values across fields during his time. Modernism does not function on such symmetry. Rather, we have ideas like the uncertainty principle, special relativity, general relativity, and the like. The idea of equality is not equal and opposite, but rather, specific and uncertain. The shift in language alone signals a true shift in the science itself as well as the societal values around it.

The first quantum theory came from Max Planck. Similar to the Doppler effect, Planck's work with blackbody radiation generated new math to prove that heat, too, functions as a propagated wave. Blackbody radiation can be seen in metalwork. Before a metal object is heated, it is completely black. As it heats, the color of the rod will change in accordance with a light spectrum—first red, then yellow, then white, and finally, blue. This is because electromagnetic waves emit at a higher and higher frequency as the heat level changes. Likewise, when the object cools, it will again be black by absorbing all of the light. This is just the first example for which classical mechanics has no mathematical explanation.

By this point in history, Einstein's thought experiments began taking shape. He spent a lot of time contemplating electromagnetic truths among other things. Einstein studied Planck's work with blackbody radiation. At that time, scientists were not sure how to measure light. They had decided that light is propagated as a wave. The first glimmer of Einstein's genius can be seen here, in quantizing light:

$E = hf$

In this case, E is energy, h represents Planck's constant (as derived from blackbody radiation), and f is frequency. This comes to stand for measuring the energy of one single photon of light.

Thus, Einstein began to demonstrate the problems of classical mechanics, which failed to account for the complexities of our universe. Although Newton's ideas are fundamental and monumentally important, Newton's theories do not hold true when applied to phenomena we cannot readily see. Einstein's explanations of quantum mechanics filled these holes in our knowledge and changed the landscape of science.

Niels Bohr was the first scientist to suggest the elliptical orbits of electrons around a nucleus in 1913.

CHAPTER 2

The Science of Quantum Theory and Mechanics

I n Einstein's initial papers and lectures introducing the theory of relativity to the public, he references some of the major mathematic discoveries in science that allowed him to fully describe relativity. Einstein's theories—special relativity and general relativity—begin as just that, theories. His writing on the subject is a play-by-play on his *gedankenexperiments*, a German word he coined to explain his so-called "thought experiments."

He presented his first idea, the theory of special relativity, in 1905. General relativity came later, in 1915. In special relativity, Einstein says that how events happen can look different to different observers; how an event is perceived in time and space is also relative to how fast the observer is moving and from where he may be observing the event. General relativity takes these ideas into account and advances them to say that space and time are two aspects of one thing (or dimension), which he calls **space-time**. He also believes space-time is curved, which relates to his understanding of gravity. Therefore, Einstein's understanding of gravity is markedly different than Newton's.

Even today, this idea of the fourth dimension sounds like science fiction. As we invent more technologies that help us make new discoveries in space, the science seems to be catching up with the fiction quite quickly. The first proof of Einstein's theories didn't come until 1919. The following section shows the mathematic and scientific discoveries that Einstein himself references in his papers as a means of explaining the logic behind relativity.

The LOGIC BEHIND RELATIVITY

Physicists were turning away from Newton's ideas in classical mechanics as Einstein was a budding scientist. Physicists, in conjunction with new inventions and technologies, were able to see more of the world than ever before. Radiography presented a way to look inside a body though X-rays. Marie Curie discovered radium shortly after the advent of radiography. These two things alone set off a series of cultural uses of radiography—from gamma ray technologies on navy ships to the eventual production of the first nuclear weapons.

Inside this field, along with optics and electrodynamics, the need to understand the mysterious consequences of light arose. Light, when isolated, allowed for these new discoveries and uses of other elements. With this ability to look in, it's no wonder that quantum mechanics was established as a new field of inquiry. As the scientists continued to look closer at the atomic and subatomic matter in the world, they observed, more precisely, mechanics. Electrons and photons weren't quite moving the way Newton predicted. And whole new ideas and experiments came to reshape our understanding of how the world works.

The most important change in science was the rise of quantum mechanics. Because Newton's "laws" no longer described the phenomena seen by scientists (often in these new technologies), new experiments and new language to describe events needed to enter the scene.

CHASING a BEAM of LIGHT

In Einstein's *Autobiographical Notes*, he recalls his first thought experiment, which we know today as "Chasing a Beam of Light." He remembers being sixteen just before the turn of the century and thinking:

> If I pursue a beam of light with the velocity c (velocity of light in a vacuum), I should observe such a beam of light as an electromagnetic field at rest though spatially oscillating.
>
> There seems to be no such thing, however, neither on the basis of experience nor according to Maxwell's equations.
>
> From the very beginning it appeared to me intuitively clear that, judged from the standpoint of such an observer, everything would have to happen according to the same laws as for an observer who, relative to the earth, was at rest. For how should the first observer know or be able to determine, that he is in a state of fast uniform motion? One sees in this paradox the germ of special relativity theory is already contained.

This thought offers us a large question physicists were contemplating at this time in history: if light is observed, would it be seen as a stream of matter (particles) or as a wave?

As more experiments occurred, they would discover that both are true. Proof of light as both matter and energy would be seen in later experiments involving the electrodynamics of a magnet, Niels Bohr's new model of the atom, the modernized **double-slit experiment** (which is still one of the great unsolved mysteries of quantum mechanics today), and more.

Light can be observed as particles *and* as waves, as seen in the double-slit experiment.

FIZEAU and the SPEED of LIGHT

Perhaps the most central idea behind Einstein's findings is that the speed of light is always constant. In order to know this absolutely, one must be able to repeatedly measure the speed of light being emitted. The first invention that captures this idea is a surprising one: photography.

The first known photograph was a heliograph taken around 1827 by Joseph Nicéphore Niépce. Niépce was making lithographic prints in order to avoid hand drawing. He was experimenting with light-sensitive varnishes and a camera. The images faded until he discovered a more stringent chemical process. When coating a pewter plate with his chemical solution and placing it in the camera, a long exposure to light allowed the image to come through and stay on the plate.

The physicist Hippolyte Fizeau wanted to improve photography. By running experiments with heat and light, he and his collaborators were able to predict many light-related phenomena.

One such prediction was **redshift**. Similar to the Doppler effect, light waves radiating from an object with different frequencies will read as different colors on a light spectrum (think of a rainbow, or a prism, in which the full continuum of colors is visible). Redshift is still a useful phenomenon in cosmology, as physicists find more and more in outer space, especially when identifying the magnitude of light coming off of a given piece of matter. For example, the light coming off of a dying star reads differently than our own sun.

Another prediction of Fizeau's was electromagnetic radiation. When thinking about the process of taking a photograph, there is visible light falling upon the subject, then there is light entering the camera and reacting with chemicals. What is it that makes light move? Fizeau's experiments suggested that electromagnetic radiation, when released, could cause visible light.

Fizeau's most important discovery, though, was to measure the speed of light itself. In 1849, Fizeau used a mirror to reflect a light beam at a spinning wheel. Though the beam was being reflected from about 8 kilometers (5 miles) away, the light hit the wheel and passed through the wheel's teeth.

Fizeau's setup of objects and light looked quite similar to a film's projection reel. By Fizeau's calculation from this experiment, he measured the speed of light to be 313,300 km/ 1 second. The number has since been refined as our ability to measure the speed has advanced. We now know the speed of light to be 299,792.458 km/1 second (186,282 miles/1 second). Fizeau's calculation would later become a prominent part of Einstein's understanding of relativity.

MAXWELL'S ELECTROMAGNETIC RADIATION

Perhaps the most relevant physicist between Newton and Einstein, James Clerk Maxwell was known for his classical theory of electromagnetic radiation. A half step between classical mechanics and quantum mechanics, his ideas brought elements like light, electricity, and magnetism into classical mechanics.

By Maxwell's measure, light could be predicted as a wave. Light, in this sense, had the same kinds of properties as sound, electricity, and magnetism. Maxwell's understanding of these phenomena allowed him to come up with ways to measure the movement of gases, to predict radio waves, and to generate the first colored photograph. His seminal work, *A Dynamical Theory of the Electromagnetic Field*, was published in 1865, just over a decade before Einstein was born.

Electrodynamics and Magnetism

Maxwell's equations, in conjunction with the known laws of classical mechanics at the time, were able to predict and show that waves of various size and magnitude were moving in the areas around electricity and magnets. Maxwell was first to describe an electromagnetic field, in which accelerated particles could have positive or negative charges. It seemed Maxwell's electromagnetic field theory followed Newton's ideas about attraction. Further, Maxwell's ideas established new math for the energy associated with these more mysterious, elemental phenomena.

As most scientists at the time believed, Maxwell's math offered explanations for motion at the subatomic and cosmic levels. His understanding of these forces abided Newton's ideas about matter that is inertial or in motion. As Einstein developed his theories of special and general relativity, he reflected upon Maxwell's electrodynamics and disagreed: if a state of rest is impossible, and the universe is in fact expanding, then Maxwell's ideas couldn't be true.

Einstein responded to the questions raised in these matters in another thought experiment, "magnet and conductor," which he explained at the onset of his 1905 lectures on special relativity. Einstein showed that in Maxwell's version of electrodynamics, a magnet at rest behaves differently than a magnet in motion.

Based on Maxwell's work, a magnet at rest is surrounded by a magnetic field, while a magnet in motion also causes an electric field to surround the magnet. By this logic, the field itself has a different, increased strength when acceleration is present.

It should seem straightforward enough that in order to prove a magnet is absolutely in motion, we would simply test to see if an electric field is present in the surrounding ether, a term that scientists used to describe a theoretical substance that surrounded the empty space around all matter that transmits radiation. In tests, though, Einstein found this does not hold true.

When a conductor or observer is added into the equation, the expected behavior is not achieved. When the magnet is in a state of rest, the conductor experiences no current (or electromagnetic wave). However, when the magnet and conductor move together, the induced electric field of the magnet cancels out that of the conductor. Thus in both cases, the observer would observe a state of rest.

This epiphany is one of the many seeds from which Einstein's theory of special relativity originates. It's one of the early thought experiments that proved to Einstein that things are relative to each other. It is in these thoughts that he began to shift the paradigm of physics thinking altogether. The notions of absolute truths in classical mechanics turned out not to be absolute at all.

Emission Theory of Light

Another important element of Maxwell's electrodynamics is how magnitudes and forces relate to light. According to Maxwell, light always propagates at a velocity c with respect to ether.

Einstein's thought experiment with the magnet and conductor proved that there is no absolute state of rest. When bringing light into the idea of relativity, Einstein found that Maxwell's claim couldn't be true here either. Light is the one element that is not relative. He would need to prove this assuredly to prove that his principle of special relativity held true in electrodynamics. Since special relativity claims that the absolutes of classical physics (mass, time, space, energy) are actually relative, the constant velocity of c can't be, as Maxwell said, relative to ether, since ether has no absolute state of rest.

LORENTZ TRANSFORMATION

The use of the **Galilean transformation** was another component of Newtonian mechanics' replacement with quantum mechanics and relativity. Newton used Galileo's coordinate system to measure things in time in space. Coordinate systems in physics are used to understand the change or transformation in space at the time of an event.

The Galilean transformation is a coordinate system based on Newton's definitions of absolute space and absolute time. Charting space and time on this coordinate system abides basic rules of geometry and algebra that we still learn in school today.

Because the speed of light is entering more of the science physicists encounter, this depiction doesn't offer enough precision. Galilean transformations don't account for the complexity of matter moving at much higher speeds—speeds near the speed of light.

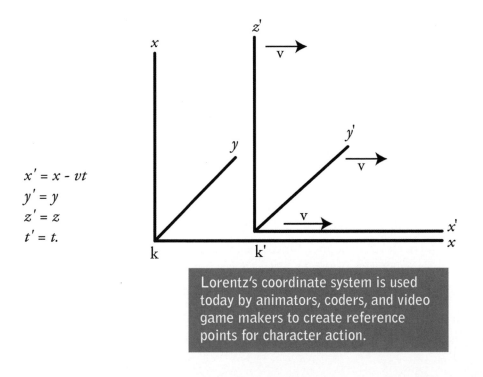

$$x' = x - vt$$
$$y' = y$$
$$z' = z$$
$$t' = t.$$

Lorentz's coordinate system is used today by animators, coders, and video game makers to create reference points for character action.

Einstein's presentation of special relativity is based on a different understanding of coordinates altogether, the **Lorentz transformation**.

Einstein refers to the time interval and the space interval represented in the Galilean transformation coordinate system as "unjustifiable hypotheses." To Einstein's contemporaries, the debunking of classical mechanics was quite radical. In order to get people to believe him, Einstein had to prove that geometry cannot account for the complex phenomena in atoms, outer space, and even (at least not precisely) on Earth.

By referring to the two-dimensional capacity of geometrics (which can be represented simply with straight lines and circles made by compasses), he then presented H. A. Lorentz's work as a counter to this Newtonian understanding of the world.

At this point in science, the Lorentz transformation offered a more dynamic understanding of motion amidst space and time. As with a train on an embankment, the coordinate system cannot be represented by one 2-D rendering. Rather, the coordinate system (or reference body) of the moving train is separate from that of the embankment it runs along. This might seem like a dense distinction. It is further explicated during Einstein's presentation of special relativity, and Einstein would not be able to prove himself without Lorentz's findings.

From the Lorentz transformation, we can see that multiple reference bodies (coordinate systems) can be understood at the same time. Further, this transformation shows that time, length, and mass of an object in motion change all by a particular factor (as shown in the patterns of the coordinate system). Known as the Lorentz factor, we know this as c, the speed of light in a vacuum. Because of Lorentz's earlier findings—that light in vacuo always propagates at c, and that the other factors of motion are relative to one another, Einstein could base his thought experiments in these math factors. The only constant thing between reference bodies is *c*.

LUMINIFEROUS ETHER

One problem scientists faced when encountering the idea of light was light-bearing matter. For example, in our everyday life, we can see and feel light being reflected and absorbed by different objects. During the summer months, when the sun is high, if you're wearing a black shirt, it will absorb more of the sun's light, and thus you'll be hotter than if you wear a white shirt. If you're wearing a white shirt, more of the sun's light will be reflected.

At the end of the nineteenth century as scientists were learning more about light through optics and electrodynamics, they wondered how and why light can move through the air at all. What ether(s) will hold light? What ether(s) will absorb it? At this time, scientists referred to such medium as luminiferous ether. The camp of scientists who hypothesized that light took the form of a wave used this as one element of proof. Since outer space and atoms have empty space, luminiferous ether proved that light could still move through it.

The Michelson and Morley Experiment

As seen in Einstein's corrections and rejections of Maxwell, luminiferous ether, too, had inconsistencies. Quantum physicists began thinking and observing that the laws of motion are relative to many factors. One question that comes from this idea as stated in Einstein's presentation of special relativity is "whether or not the motion of earth in space can be made perceptible in terrestrial experiments." Einstein tells his readers about Michelson and Morley's famous experiment, which involved two mirrors that

A large object can distort space-time, especially the larger its mass.

faced one another. Michelson and Morley timed the reflection of light between the two mirrors under different circumstances, attempting to calculate the effect of the ether. The failure of the Michelson-Morley experiment (MMX) was that there was no ether. Thus, light does not rely on ether to move.

It is difficult to imagine this, but if we think back to Lorentz, we remember that each reference body has its own relativity. MMX did not find a difference between the speed of light relative to the direction it moved in. This negative result helped Einstein prove that the speed of light is absolute, regardless of other phenomena and events that happen in time and space.

MINKOWSKI'S 4-D SPACE

A central idea to relativity is that space and time exist as a space-time continuum. It is still very counterintuitive to understand this in our reality. We can begin to see how Einstein arrived at this deconstruction of time and space from the failures of Newtonian mechanics, as well as the Lorentz transformation. Once we start seeing multiple reference bodies interact, we begin to understand that the measure of time and space is relative to each separate coordinate system. This becomes easier to see when considering outer space and/or atomic and subatomic particles (because motion is more exaggerated in those two spaces than in our day-to-day life).

Hermann Minkowski was one of Einstein's teachers. Based on what Einstein was developing in his theory of special relativity, Minkowski realized the ideas needed a new medium to be placed upon. In Newton's mind, space was a stage with an absolute axis representing space and an absolute axis representing time. Special relativity suggested that neither of those phenomena were absolute at all.

Minkowski hypothesized that you could use a Lorentz transformation to rotate any given coordinates into an imagined four-dimensional space. He suggested that you could use three "real" coordinates (as you would normally) and one imagined coordinate to represent the fourth dimension.

According to Minkowski's space, space and time are inextricably linked. If you take one step forward, you've moved in space. It is also true that when you took that step, a certain amount of time passed. In this sense, you cannot measure space without measuring it relative to time, and vice versa.

Minkowski's four-dimensional space is an essential idea behind Einstein's idea of space-time. The continuum will show further examples of how the link between time and space can't be unbraided from our measurements and understandings of large phenomena.

It is difficult for us to imagine space-time, even now. We perceive ourselves as being in motion or at rest. We are very small compared to the phenomena around us, though. Even when we are asleep, Earth is spinning, Earth rotates around the sun, and the moon rotates around Earth. There is no such state as "at rest."

GAUSSIAN COORDINATES

In the early 1800s, Carl Friedrich Gauss realized a system of coordinates that suggested a more advanced geometry than what the world knew before.

Within the curved lines of Gauss's coordinate system, we can begin to understand the idea of infinity, and even **multiple sets of infinity**. The figure shows multiple curved lines that do not intersect, each labeled u with a subsequent number. Between any two of the curves, we should be able to draw an

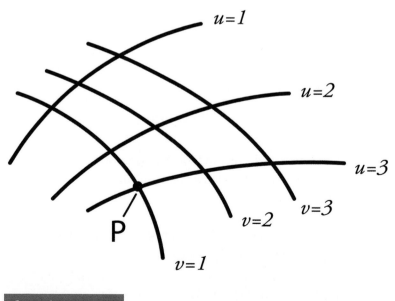

Gauss's system

infinite number of lines, which correspond to real numbers. The same is true of the v curves.

To imagine this clearly, let's think for a moment of a standard ruler. On the ruler, 12 inches are marked off in order from 1 to 12. Between each inch, we have a marking at the ½ inch. Between the ½ inch and whole inch, we have a slightly shorter marking that gives us a ¼ inch. Between the ¼ and ½ inch is a slightly shorter line marking ⅛ inch. And between the ⅛-inch markings and the ¼-inch markings is an even shorter marking for the 1/16-inch quantities.

If we keep zooming in on sections of the ruler, we can continue to put points on a line. This tells us two things about infinity. First, we can count to infinity in whole numbers: 1, 2, 3, 4, 5, 6, and so on, until we reach infinity. We can call this an infinite set. Second, when considering the points between whole numbers, as with our ruler, we can place notches between each real number infinitely. This is a second, larger, infinite set. Though it seems counterintuitive that there could be an infinity that is somehow larger than another, we've just proved it with a basic example from our reality.

When we do this same thing between Gaussian coordinates and apply it to three and four dimensions, we begin to see Einstein's theories of special and general relativity. On Gaussian coordinates, Einstein writes:

> Gauss invented a method for the mathematical treatment of continua in general, in which "size-relations" ("distances" between neighboring points) are defined. To every point of a continuum are assigned as many numbers (Gaussian co-ordinates) as the continuum has dimensions.

Einstein needed the Lorentz transformation, Minkowski's four-dimensional space, and Gaussian

Hermann Minkowski: 1864–1909

An important figure in Einstein's life was his teacher Hermann Minkowski. In order for the scientific paradigm to shift from classical mechanics to the quantum universe, Einstein had to theorize and prove that time and space are utterly different than our experience of them. Without Minkowski, Einstein could not have done this.

Minkowski was a Polish Jew born in 1864. He became Germanized at a young age when his family left Poland to escape Russian persecution and found solace in Königsberg. Minkowski's father, Lewin, ended up working in manufacturing. Lewin worked on mechanical clockwork inside of toys. Lewin's work may have inspired his son's work in number theory, and later, Hermann's most notable contribution to science, Minkowski's space-time.

Minkowski was educated in Germany. He ended up teaching in many places, including Zurich, where he met a young Albert Einstein. Later, Minkowski recognized the possibilities of Einstein's ideas. Between special relativity and general relativity, Minkowski encouraged Einstein to think of time and space as woven. Eventually, Minkowski used the work of Einstein, Lorentz, and Henri Poincaré to argue that there could be a fourth dimension. This idea of 4-D time and space was radical, hard to imagine (it still is), and as it turns out, correct.

Minkowski died young. When he was forty-four, he died of appendicitis. He had been married to Auguste Adler. They had two daughters: Lily in 1898 and Ruth in 1902. Hermann Minkowski's great contributions to our current understanding of space-time have not been forgotten.

coordinates to unveil his ideas about space and time as
a space-time continuum. As seen from his ideas about
Gaussian coordinates, when applied to multiple dimensions,
things stay infinitely dense. In space, this suggests a set of
infinite coordinates, or rather, a reference body that can
grow into infinity. The thinking of these scientists helps us
see today not only that Einstein's theories of relativity are
true, but that they predict larger truths about the universe;
namely, that it is, in fact, expanding.

BOHR ATOM

Other scientists helped Einstein refine his ideas after he had
already conceived of special relativity. Niels Bohr is one such
scientist. His work with the atom shaped Einstein's notion of
general relativity.

One important difference between the science in the
theory of special relativity and the theory of general relativity
is the attention to gravity. In 1905, when Einstein presented his
ideas about special relativity, he was able to debunk classical
mechanics step-by-step. He focused mostly on proving that
the speed of light is finite and constant, and because of that
absolute truth, other factors of observing an event in the
universe—small or large—are relative to that alone. In order to
build the complexity of the theory for grander understanding
and prove to the world that an unseen fourth dimension,
space-time, existed, he needed to bring the role of gravity back
into the conversation.

When he re-presented gravity in his own terms, it
couldn't have the same role as it once did on Newton's stages
of absolute time and absolute space. Instead, it had to be
relative to space-time as measured by the constant speed
of light.

Before Einstein arrived at general relativity in 1915,
Niels Bohr presented a new model of the atom. Physicists in

electrodynamics, optics, and the growing field of quantum mechanics already began applying Einstein's ideas of special relativity to their work. They also used the Lorentz transformation, the Lorentz factor (the constant velocity c for the speed of light), and these other building blocks of quantum physics to continue understanding atoms, subatomic particles, and cosmology. By applying the new ideas, they were able to correct and expand upon the prior knowledge.

In 1913, Bohr presented a model of an atom. His model included a new finding about electrons. Based on Newton's work, scientists believed that an atom functioned like a mini universe. Just like the sun with planets in perfect orbit, a nucleus at the center of an atom was orbited by subatomic particles—protons, neutrons, and electrons. But through relativity and electrodynamics, Bohr found something mysterious about electrons: they do not always keep their orbit as predicted.

Instead, when an atom absorbs or emits energy, its electrons can move between orbits. When the electron jumps, Bohr observed that it emits a photon. Although the Bohr model doesn't explain everything about why the electron can behave this way, it paved the way for many crucial scientific changes to come: the invention of the atomic bomb, Heisenberg's uncertainty principle, and a model of inspiration for Einstein's general relativity when applied to gravitational fields.

Albert Einstein once said, "If I weren't a physicist, I would probably be a musician."

CHAPTER 3

The Major Players in Quantum Mechanics

Albert Einstein is a household name across cultures and societies. And despite the complexity and richness of his contributions, the majority of his theories belong to him alone. Relativity is a prime example.

Einstein's relativity paved the way for a fully realized field of quantum mechanics and **atomic physics**. Relativity additionally advanced and reshaped cosmology and **astrophysics**. Einstein's work figures heavily into the fabric of the twentieth century because his scientific discoveries (and subsequent inventions) determined his ability to escape his homeland, Germany, during the Nazi regime. Because of his escape, Einstein was able to continue to work, resulting eventually in the invention of the atomic bomb.

While Einstein is the sole dreamer of relativity itself, there are other players bound up in the history of Einstein's work. To undo classical mechanics, a whole field of physicists needed to transform quantum theory from mere theory into quantum mechanics. This chapter first looks at those scientists responsible for the transformation before taking a closer look at Albert Einstein's life and contributions.

Like Einstein, Planck loved music: he sang and played piano, organ, and cello.

MAX PLANCK, FATHER of QUANTUM THEORY

Einstein—like many geniuses, artists, and great thinkers—failed at the beginning of his career. Unable to find a teaching job after school, he took a post as a patent clerk in Switzerland for a few years. In that time, he had a few small papers published about Maxwell's work. It wasn't until the very well-known scientist Max Planck (1858–1947) believed in his ideas that Einstein would be able to rise to his eventual fame.

Planck was a famous German scholar in his own right. As scientists were able to study the atom more closely, Planck became skeptical of the atom. Could it behave only as a particle? Could it only be measured as a particle? Especially since subatomic particles showed kinetic and energetic movement around a nucleus, it seemed to Planck that the theories of classical mechanics could not hold.

Planck's refutation of classical mechanics came in the form of a new constant, h. Planck's constant h is used to describe the curvature of radiation when light is absorbed or reflected. By implementing this idea of curvature to measure and understand the behavior of emitted light, Planck was the first to turn the field against particle theory and toward wave mechanics, eventually leading to quantum theory and the field of quantum mechanics as we know it today.

Planck's constant is his legacy, and the idea led to a Nobel Prize in Physics in 1918. Throughout his life, Max Planck was a well-respected scientist. His theories were celebrated. Yet Planck's personal life was full of hardship. He outlived his first wife and four of his children.

Planck and Blackbody Radiation

When Einstein's first three essays about special relativity were published, he was an unknown young scientist with ideas that countered entire fields of science. From electrodynamics to classical mechanics, his proposals suggested we inherited a rusty machine from Newton—a universe that was too basic to account for all the elegant behaviors of matter, from atoms to stars to other unnamed, massive objects in the cosmos.

Planck recognized the importance of special relativity immediately from this unknown genius. Just before the turn of the twentieth century, he was commissioned by electrical companies to do work with lightbulbs. The hope was that

Planck could find a way to use even less energy and generate more (brighter) light from a bulb.

Though Planck didn't achieve his aim, during his blackbody radiation experiment, he did arrive at Planck's constant. Planck's research influenced Einstein greatly. Like Einstein, Planck intuited that classical mechanics wrongly described many phenomena in the universe. In particular, it had been the great effort of physics to quantify things as being absolute—in behavior and measurement. Time was absolute and could be measured in ticks of a clock. Space was absolute and could be measured in paces on any standardized ruler. And likewise, matter could be measured in its visible three dimensions and maintain those measures absolutely.

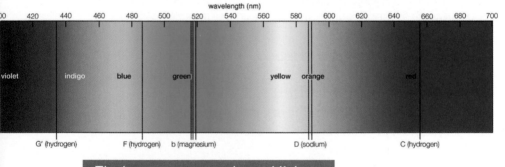

The human eye can only read light at certain wavelengths along the visible light spectrum.

Although this matches our day-to-day understanding of time, space, and objects, the advances and inventions of science at the time allowed people like Planck to observe matter more closely. By looking at an atom, one could find the atom's subatomic particles. And those particles were moving around a nucleus. If we were to keep splitting matter open, one would keep finding these patterns—fractals, which repeated their shapes to scale. It seemed to Planck that nothing could be at absolute rest. Further, he saw that light couldn't be observed or measured the same way that a particle was observed or measured.

Many like-minded scientists had the same thought. Is matter made up of particles? Or were these findings about electromagnetic fields, light, and other phenomena telling us something else? Are things a continuous wave? Does energy radiate as a tide? Does matter simply interrupt the dance?

During his experiments, Planck decided to investigate hot metal. When certain material reaches high heats, it gives off a glow—specifically, when metal is very hot, it gives off a red glow. On the spectrum of light, this red is the highest "reading" that we can see and understand. It's a measure of the light's magnitude or intensity.

Planck and his colleagues, under the guidance of another famous physicist, Gustav Kirchoff, used a closed metal container with a tiny hole in it to measure the intensity of light. Metal is a great absorber of light. That's why the hottest temperatures yield a red glow from, say, an iron rod. When light escaped from the hole, depending on the temperature of the metal, it would fall in a wavelength, which Kirchoff and his team would graph.

Kirchoff died without the answer to his most relevant question: "How does the intensity of electromagnetic radiation emitted by a blackbody depend on the frequency of the radiation and the temperature of the body?"

Planck guessed that the curvature of these lines followed specific patterns (his constant). Similar to the Doppler effect, Planck figured that the waves could be quantized. Even if the thing being emitted was a wave, certainly the curvature and frequency could be predicted and measured. By using a constant to stand in for the radiated heat of an object, the resulting frequency could show the energy of the event. Planck suggested:

$$E = h\nu$$

where the constant multiplied by the frequency of radiated waves would give you the energy, or the resulting color on the light spectrum.

This constant, which was mysterious to Planck at the time, marks the birth of quantum physics. The philosophy behind this constant shows a turn from particle theory to an interest in wave mechanics. This shift allowed Einstein's intuitions to be grounded, at least somewhat, before being ultimately proved by phenomena in the universe.

Planck took Kirchoff's post at Berlin University just as an unknown patent clerk's early papers on relativity were published. Planck and Einstein built a relationship as colleagues in science. They had conversations about the merits (or lack thereof) of classical mechanics. During the first winds of relativity, these two brilliant and stubborn men argued about science often. Their critical inquiry led them to deep conversations about Maxwell's electrodynamics. Eventually, Einstein convinced Planck that Maxwell's work in electrodynamics followed classical mechanics, and therefore, didn't explain the behaviors of magnetism and electricity precisely enough.

Planck's post at Berlin University allowed him to create a professorship for Einstein. Despite their differences in personality, their temperaments allowed their arguments to move toward a conservative articulation of quantum theory. By the 1920s the two would stand together against atomic physicists in their proposition of quantum mechanics, even. Their camaraderie was crucial to the field of quantum mechanics. The two men and a few other scientists were known to play music together in their free time at Planck's estate. Einstein was a lover of the violin, especially.

EINSTEIN and HENDRIK ANTOON LORENTZ

H. A. Lorentz's work was the most immediately crucial to Einstein's special and general theories of relativity. Lorentz's transformation proved that multiple reference bodies needed to be accounted for in understanding a given event. His constant *c* for the speed of light in vacuo helped Einstein prove his theories.

Einstein used so much of Lorentz's work as the mathematical explanation for his thought experiments that the first versions of his essays were published with both of their names on it; special relativity was even called Lorentz-Einstein Theory.

After Einstein's initial presentation of special relativity in 1905, Lorentz supported Einstein by incorporating special relativity into his work with electrons. He affirmatively referenced Einstein's ideas in his own publications.

Hendrik Antoon Lorentz's contributions to many fields within physics earned him a Nobel Prize.

Lorentz also, from the start, encouraged Einstein to develop the general theory of relativity. He publicly stated that Einstein's theories were a triumph when the total eclipse of 1919 offered the first proof of general relativity to the world.

Einstein also loved Lorentz greatly. In 1928, he wrote of Lorentz:

> The enormous significance of his work consisted therein, that it forms the basis for the theory of atoms and for the general and special theories of relativity. The special theory was a more detailed expose of those concepts which are found in Lorentz's research of 1895.

Lorentz died the same year this letter was written. Einstein gave his eulogy. Later in Einstein's life, two years before he himself died, he wrote of Lorentz: "For me personally he meant more than all the others I have met on my life's journey." Lorentz was beloved by the whole of the scientific community.

ALBERT EINSTEIN, HIMSELF

Albert Einstein was a German Jew born in 1879. He lived until 1955, when he died of an aneurism. He was one of the most prolific thinkers of the twentieth century, and arguably of all time. During his life, he published more than three hundred scientific papers. He also published many works in other genres.

Though the world wouldn't know him until later, his genius was recognized by the time he was merely sixteen. In his *Autobiographical Notes*, he recalls his first thought experiment, in which he imagines what he might see if he tried to chase a light beam.

This memory is the seed of his most important work, the theory of relativity. Both special and general relativity rely on

Einstein's Letters to Max Born

Albert Einstein's friendship with the German physicist Max Born has been preserved through a collection of letters between the pair. The letters demonstrate Einstein's triumphs and frustrations as he developed his theories:

> I find quite intolerable the idea that an electron exposed to radiation should choose of its own free will, not only its moment to jump off but also its direction. In that case, I'd rather be a cobbler, or an employee in a gaming-house than a physicist.

The letters also show Einstein's view of himself, his work habits, and his warm friendships with other scientists. Perhaps the most interesting aspect of his letters is how even Einstein was not immune from day-to-day concerns:

> ... I must revise my book on relativity, as Springer intends to issue a second edition; but I will not get round to it this term. If you have spotted any errors or omissions, I should be grateful for the information. Pauli's article for the Encyclopaedia is apparently finished, and the weight of the paper is said to be 2½ kilos. This should give some indication of its intellectual weight. The little chap is not only clever but industrious as well.
>
> I've had some fun here recently, in the form of a substantial burglary. The rogues broke in at night through a cellar window after breaking the bars, and got away with a lot of silver, linen, both bicycles, and even my suit and shoes from the first floor.

the constant speed of light as one of the only (if not *the* only) absolute factors of the universe.

Like many geniuses, Einstein's daydreaming was his most fruitful habit. In his work on relativity, he first describes riding a train. He spends page after page returning to this simple image of a train in motion along an embankment. He imagines it from every instance and standpoint. He returns to the image with new ideas and math to measure our reality against. Though reading *Relativity: The Special and General Theory* is difficult, slow, and at times, dense, it is his dogma, his relentless returning to the thought experiment that keeps us on board the train with him.

Einstein's Personal Affairs

When Einstein was a young student in Zurich, there was one woman among the seven students in the mathematics department, Mileva Marić. Marić and Einstein eventually became romantically involved. Before they married, they had a daughter named Lieserl. It is unknown whether their daughter died or was given up for adoption. Lieserl was not known to the public until the late 1980s when many of Einstein's letters were published. In his letters to Marić while she was staying with her parents away from Zurich, Lieserl's existence was disclosed. The two later married and had two sons.

After special relativity, Einstein's marriage worsened. By 1914, the two scientists separated. The boys returned to Zurich with their mother while Einstein stayed in Berlin. Einstein and Marić divorced in 1919, the same year general relativity made Einstein world famous and the same year that he remarried. Some say that Marić was not a failed mathematician, but rather, that she may have collaborated with Einstein on his 1905 publications, though this theory is not widely accepted.

Einstein harbored an earlier love, a woman named Marie Winteler, during his marriage to Marić. His letters reveal that he was confessing his love to her in 1910 while he was still in his first marriage. He then began seeing his cousin Elsa Löwenthal around 1912. They married in 1919 once Einstein's divorce with Marić was official. Einstein and Löwenthal didn't have children of their own, though Löwenthal's daughters from her first marriage changed their name and considered Einstein their father.

The two moved to America in 1933. Just before their move, Einstein's youngest son, Eduard, had a schizophrenic breakdown. Marić was left to care for him after he became institutionalized. Einstein had set up a fund for Marić and his two sons after winning the Nobel Prize in 1922. He continued to make financial contributions to this fund while he was in America.

Einstein's second wife died of heart and kidney problems shortly after moving to America. During her excruciating three-year-long illness and the time after, Einstein kept himself involved in his work, hoping to resolve his heartbreak.

Dogma

As much as Einstein was known for being a daydreamer—a mad scientist, with his head in the clouds—he was also very stubborn. He believed that the laws of physics should articulate natural phenomena. They could not be law if they did not hold true across states of nature.

When his ideas first entered the world, this stubbornness both helped and hurt his case for relativity. Scientists who were far more well known and established didn't have a reason to believe Einstein. The geniuses before Einstein all agreed upon classical mechanics. And in newer fields like electrodynamics, the inconsistencies would eventually work themselves out under the same laws of mechanics as every other field had done since Newton.

Stubbornness can also be read as arrogance. Einstein disagreed vehemently with his initial PhD advisor about many things in science. Before Einstein even conceived of relativity, he felt his advisor was behind the times in his thinking and demanded that the university give him another mentor.

While some turned away from Einstein at his initial presentation of relativity, those who were interested in it were ready to engage with him. In the academic world, this engagement meant productive arguing and questioning. Especially since Einstein's ideas were dreamt up theories without lab reports and math to go with them, he needed to have rigorous conversations to solidify his thoughts, generate the math to go with the ideas, and encourage others to accept relativity. By sticking to his intuitions, relentlessly, he was able to achieve the ultimate goal: to understand the universe with more precise eyes and to teach others to do the same.

Pacifism and Activism

Einstein was known for his pacifism and activism during his life. While he was still in Europe, he stood by his antiwar stance. Because of Einstein's clout, he was able to get out of Germany during the reign of the Nazis. The Nazis banned Jews from all teaching positions at universities. When Einstein found out about this, he wrote to university leaders in other countries begging them to take in unemployed German-Jewish professors of science. His letter saved one thousand German-Jewish scientists, who were taken in by Turkey.

Einstein lived as a refugee in America. He later worked with the NAACP and relevant African American figures of the era to combat racism in the United States. It makes sense that as a man exiled from his country, he would fight racism in his new land. He even referred to America's racism as its "worst disease."

Since WWII, scientists on the brink of great discoveries have engaged in conflict by necessity.

The Manhattan
Project physicists

The Manhattan Project

In 1939, it became clear that the Germans were working on
a nuclear weapon. Their interest in uranium, in particular,
tipped off scientists and the intelligence community. Einstein
collaborated with Leo Szilard on a letter to President Roosevelt
urging him to beat Germany to the punch. Roosevelt funded
and established the Manhattan Project as a means to develop
an atomic weapon before the Germans could.

Despite Einstein's longstanding pacifism, the mass
genocide of European Jews in conjunction with science led
him to activism in the form of invention. The dire situation
of WWII convinced him, in the end, to fight for his cause.
A group of atomic physicists met in secret to develop the
first atomic weapon at a facility in Los Alamos, New Mexico,

under the guidance of J. Robert Oppenheimer. Though German scientists arrived at nuclear fission first, it is this team of scientists in the US who were first to make an atomic bomb. Their work led to dropping two nuclear bombs on Japan, a decision of much controversy to human rights, modes of war, and ethics.

RELATIVITY: An INDIVIDUAL EFFORT?

In spite of the fact that the theories of general and special relativity belong exclusively to Einstein, it is undeniable that Einstein's work depended on the work of his contemporaries—and his scientific forebears. Einstein's massive contribution relied on several key players. Towering figures like Planck, Maxwell, Lorentz, and others pushed Einstein. These figures challenged his ideas and stimulated his imagination.

In the one hundred years since Einstein's theory became public, we've added technology like this GPS floating through space-time.

CHAPTER 4

The Discovery Itself

Unlike many scientists, Einstein used logic, math, and description to articulate his ideas, versus spending time in a lab. At first, this way of convincing the public of new science didn't quite work. Time would have to pass to give scientific proof to the ideas. Because his thought experiments are so precise and vivid, when rereading them these days, the genius is in the clarity. Also, because we have more technologies entering the market every day that help us understand life beyond Earth, the relevance of his thought experiments has grown exponentially. We know more about relativity now than Einstein ever could have guessed would be true.

Another important shift from the past to Einstein is the word "theory" itself. Whereas Newton referred to his ideas as "rules," "laws," and "principles," Einstein did not. Newton's word choices impose "absolute" truth onto the ideas. As scientists began to see these things fail through new discoveries, it was clear that seeking the absolute was less relevant than seeking the uncertain. Time and space would no longer be absolute. The uncertainty principle and the theory of relativity would be aptly named to show the infinite expanse and wonder that comes with scientific discovery both at the subatomic and cosmic levels.

The SPECIAL THEORY of RELATIVITY

Einstein's essays and lectures begin with the special theory of relativity in 1905. Einstein says that time is relative to motion. This claim goes against classical mechanics, as shaped by Newton's notions of absolute time and absolute space. To begin, we need to first understand the difference between what is absolute and what is relative.

If we return to our earlier example of a train going between Chicago and Deerfield, Illinois, we can see the difference between these two ideas. If someone is sitting on a train going from Chicago, north, to Deerfield, Lake Michigan will be on her right. If another person takes the train from Deerfield to Chicago, Lake Michigan will be on that observer's left. The placement of the lake is relative to the observer. Now let's say it's wintertime and the lake is frozen. Regardless of if the lake is to the observer's left or right, all observers would be able to agree that the lake is frozen, making it an absolute statement.

Choosing the train example is intentional as a train is one of the central images to Einstein's gedankenexperiments. In Einstein's work on special relativity, he begins with the following basic example:

> I stand at the window of a railway carriage which is travelling uniformly, and drop a stone on the embankment, without throwing it. Then, disregarding the influence of the air resistance, I see the stone descend in a straight line. A pedestrian who observes the misdeed from the footpath notices that the stone falls to earth in a parabolic curve. I now ask: Do the "positions" traversed by the stone lie "in reality" on a straight line or on a parabola? Moreover, what is meant here by motion "in space"?

Here, Einstein begins to break down the problem of absolutes in classical mechanics, which don't allow an accurate measurement of motion because they don't account for the relativity of each observer. It's important that he begins with this dense example because it also makes claims against basic geometry. We are used to measuring rigid points on a rigid graph of coordinates (or, a reference body). Einstein is layering in motion what is unaccounted for by basic geometry, which was the seed of classical mechanics. He continues:

> We imagine two clocks of identical construction; the man at the railway-carriage window is holding one of them, and the man on the footpath the other. Each of the observers determines the position on his own reference-body occupied by the stone at each tick of the clock he is holding in his hand. In this connection we have not taken account of the inaccuracy involved by the finiteness of the velocity of propagation of light [...]

He has already set up complexities that classical mechanics do not have the answer to. For example, he's suggested that only two things are "absolute": the fact that the clocks are identical and the "finiteness" of the speed of light. The latter wouldn't even be properly accounted for until ten years later when he presented general relativity. In the meantime, it's important to hold this setup in mind as we consider altering our understanding of the relationships between space, time, and motion. What we would normally draw on a 2-D coordinate system in geometry and classical physics now needs to be reconsidered. The reference body of the moving train will not be the same as the embankment that it rides along. Neither will it be the same as the footpath of the second observer. Having created a model, Einstein would present mathematic considerations to replace our prior physics equations with (and/or ideas to consider simultaneously).

The Principle of Relativity

As described in his initial thought experiment, Einstein had to account for his intuitions about the relations (see how "relate" is part of that word and "relativity"?!) between space, time, and motion without yet regarding the finiteness of the speed of light. One way to consider these ideas is in vacuo, or, in outer space, without gravitational influence.

Einstein took his train example up into space. Imagine two observers in space suits. Each is inside her own space station. In free space, there is no acceleration, rotation, or gravitation. Let's say each space station has its own clocks and measuring rods. The clocks (as in the train example) are made identically. In his seminal work, Einstein refers to these observers as **"inertial observers."**

In the case of these two observers, there are a series of questions we can ask about what is relative and what is absolute. Since we are imagining free space, let's say the first observer sees the second observer and her space station pass by with what she perceives as a great speed. For the second observer though, it is the first space station and observer that are in motion while she is at rest, or inert. In this situation, motion and rest are relative to each observer. In this case, *velocity* is the relative factor.

In this setup, Einstein suggests another flaw in Newton's work: there is no known absolute state of rest. On our own coordinate system, or reference body, we consider absolute rest based on our perception of time and space. However, Earth is in constant motion on its own reference body. In this version of the universe, the planets have their own reference bodies, and thus, their own gravitational fields. It's why he must exercise the thought experiment in space, not just in reality.

Because there is no known "absolute rest," Einstein arrives at a clear principle of relativity:

Whenever an inertial observer in her space station performs an experiment, any other inertial observer who has constructed exactly the same experimental setup in her own space station will get the same result.

Because we are still considering a world in vacuo, it seems more believable that so much is relative to the observer, including space and time. Einstein's theories of relativity are especially powerful because he states that in order to make claims about these phenomena, they must hold true at both the quantum level as well as the cosmic one. Therefore, when placing these observers and objects back into our model of a train moving along an embankment, these special rules of relativity should still hold true according to the reference bodies of the observers within our gravitational field(s).

The Relativity of Simultaneity

Einstein's theory and principle of special relativity suggest, among other things, that simultaneity is relative. Einstein furthers his thought experiment about the train to begin breaking down the nature of time in physics.

Lightning has struck the rails on our railway embankment at two places *A* and *B* far distant from each other. I make the additional assertion that these two lightning flashes occurred simultaneously.

Einstein then talks directly to the reader. He says by current logic, one would agree with him as the idea seems simple enough. But if we look closely at the math and science needed to apply this to our reality, we run into a few problems. At first it would seem we could prove the simultaneity by making a line between *A* and *B*. Then, the observer should be placed at the midpoint, *M*. Einstein suggests, then, that the observer should be given two mirrors—one for each end point of the line—placed at 90° angles, so both points can be seen by the observer at the same time.

Einstein then discounts this as being exact by pointing out that we'd also need to measure for sure that the light of the lightning flash at each point travels with the same velocity as the other ($A \rightarrow M = B \rightarrow M$).

At this point, relativity suggests that we still have two recurring problems: the propagation (or speed) of light and measuring time. In order to rethink "time" in physics, Einstein sets up clocks in his thought experiment:

> For this purpose we suppose that clocks of identical construction are placed at the points *A*, *B*, and *C* of the railway line (co-ordinate system), and that they are set in such a manner that the positions of their pointers are simultaneously the same. Under these conditions we understand by the "time" of an event the reading (position of the hands) of that one of these clocks which is in the immediate vicinity (in space) of the event. In this manner a time-value is associated with every event, which is essentially capable of observation.
>
> This stipulation contains a further physical hypothesis[…][:] When two clocks arranged at rest in different places of a reference-body are set in such a manner that a particular position of the pointers of the one clock is simultaneous (in the above sense) with the same position of the pointers of the other clock, then identical "settings" are always simultaneous.

So far, so good. Einstein explains the way time should work in a physical sense. We've set up some basic rules and parameters. But when we go back to the train moving along the embankment, he points us to the next immediate problem: Are the two strokes of lightning, which are simultaneous with reference to the railway embankment, also simultaneous relatively to the train?

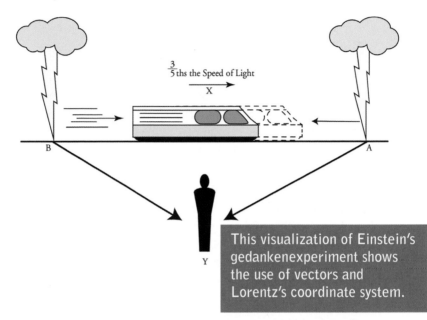

$\frac{3}{5}$ths the Speed of Light

X

B

A

This visualization of Einstein's gedankenexperiment shows the use of vectors and Lorentz's coordinate system.

Y

The velocity of the train (upon which is the observer) must be accounted for when judging the possibility of simultaneity. Given the embankment as a reference body and the velocity of the train and observer moving toward point B, the observer sees the beam of light in front of the train *earlier* than the beam of light behind the train. This brings Einstein to an important revelation:

Events which are simultaneous with reference to the embankment are not simultaneous with respect to the train, and vice versa (**relativity of simultaneity**). Every reference-body (co-ordinate system) has its own particular time; unless we are told the reference-body to which the statement of time refers, there is no meaning in a statement of the time of an event.

It is here, within the theory of special relativity, that Einstein has undone the world of Newton's absolute time. In very simple terms, he has proven that the overlay of reference bodies can't be ignored when conducting the mathematics of physics.

The Relativity of Space

Thus far in his explanation of special relativity, Einstein has established that motion is relative to the observer and that every reference body (or system of coordinates) has its own time. Further, he's given examples of how time is relative to the state of motion of a given reference body (say, a moving train, or the spin of a planet …). The last piece of this puzzle is to prove that space is also relative to an observer.

Einstein gets back on the train in his thought experiment. He describes that to measure distance, there are two approaches. First, he suggests using the train itself as the reference body. That an observer could take his measuring rod from the front of the first train (point $A1$), marking off—in a straight line—as many times as necessary until the end of the last train (point $B1$). So far, it seems like basic geometry and physics could answer this problem: the distance between A and B would equal a certain distance, w. However, in special relativity, we have to give consideration to the other elements of reference body (in this case, the train).

Einstein elaborates by thinking, instead, we were measuring the distance of the front of the train to the back of the train from the reference body of the railway. From this point of view, $A1$ and $B1$ are moving at a certain velocity (v). Einstein claims that first, you'd need to find the coordinate points, A and B of the embankment, which points $A1$ and $B1$ will pass at a particular time (t) *as judged from the embankment*. Einstein has taken back into the logical circle of relativity. Because the amount of time it takes the train to pass points A and B as seen from the embankment could be different than the amount of time (*t1*) it takes the observer to measure points *A1* to *B1* on a moving train, the only conclusion available is a relative one:

> If the man in the carriage covers the distance *w* in a unit of time—measured from the train—then this distance—as measured from the embankment—is not necessarily also equal to *w*.

Though some of these conclusions seem counterintuitive, observing each reference body under its own terms begins to build complex truths, which can be applied to both quantum mechanics and cosmology. Namely, Einstein's ability to bring such large ideas into mechanics—ideas that deny and refute the authority of Newtonian mechanics—presents the world with our current understanding of the universe: that the universe is expanding, and within it, space and time *correlate* (there's that root again—relation, relative, etc.) with each other and are not separate and absolute entities.

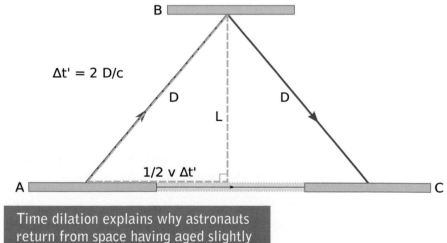

Time dilation explains why astronauts return from space having aged slightly less than they would have on Earth.

One mathematic conclusion that comes from the relativity of simultaneity and the relativity of space is Einstein's **time dilation**. Time dilation is the difference of elapsed time between events as measured by different observers. This applies to every example so far—the observer who throws a stone off the railway carriage, and the one on the footpath below; the two astronauts on different space stations; the distance between train cars as measured from the moving train and from the embankment; and so on.

Clocks as Reference Bodies

Einstein took the Lorentz transformation and figured out just how to make it accountable for space-time, as the two can no longer be represented as separate absolutes. The Lorentz transformation considers points as Cartesian coordinates do, which is to say, rigidly (or, at rest). Einstein figured out that the "rods" that make up a given reference frame might not be at rest or in vacuo. He imagined that a given rod functions in the same way that a hand on a clock does. A reference frame moving in space, therefore, would need to consider the time it takes a rod to "tick" as in a clock hand. If we place this idea back into Einstein's thought experiment with the train, it holds true that the clock with the observer on the train goes more slowly than the one at rest with the man on the footpath, who watches the stone fall.

The RESULTS of SPECIAL RELATIVITY to the FIELD at LARGE

The key result of these findings within special relativity is a correction to formerly believed mechanics. In classical physics, conservation of energy and conservation of mass are rigid, fundamental laws. In Newton's math, the laws are independent of each other. But through relativity, Einstein concludes they are all present in one law.

Unlike classical mechanics, in which a coordinate system always has the same absolute properties of time and space (think of algebra and geometry: imagine drawing lines and parabolas on graph paper, in which the x and y axis are represented the same way…), relativity "requires that the law of the conservation of energy should hold not only with reference to a coordinate system K, but also with respect to every coordinate system, $K1$ which is in a state of uniform motion of translation relative to K."

What Einstein means here is that each reference body must hold a law of conservation of energy to be true. The Lorentz transformation is one way to understand how to get from one reference body to another and compare the relativity of objects and observers. The example of clocks ticking is one way to see that if the rule is the same from one clock to another, then the *difference* should be found by holding the reference bodies relative to each other.

Special relativity comes mostly from electrodynamics and optics. In these fields, the speed of light matters theoretically and in the practical application of technologies at the time. These levels of relativity work from taking X-rays all the way down to observing how an atom works.

The Speed of Light as Finite

Another result of special relativity is that the speed of light is not relative. Based on the Lorentz transformation and Lorentz factor, we can begin to see that while everything else is relative, the speed of light is not.

If we return to our train running between Chicago and Deerfield, we can see special relativity at work. If the train is speeding along at 110 mph from Chicago to Deerfield, and a car beside the tracks is going the same speed, then the observers in each respective vehicle would claim the other car does not move (or at least, doesn't change). Now, we know that if we are driving in a car at 110 mph, we will likely be arrested, so let's say the car is going 65 mph while the train continues along at 110 mph. Relative to the observer in the car, the train forges ahead at 45 mph.

Based on these cases, it would seem that we could simply do the same—add or subtract velocities—for our two astronauts floating in free space on their different space stations. Let's say the first astronaut sees a light signal given off of the second space station and measures its velocity to be the constant 299,792.458 km/1 second. If she then sees the second astronomer chasing that same beam of light, based on our example with the car and the train, we should be able to measure her velocity and subtract it from the speed of the first light signal. Let's imagine that the first astronaut measures it based on the speed of the light signal the space station gives off when accelerating toward the first light beam. It appears that the second space station moves at half the speed of the first light signal. Based on the example with the train and car, we should be able to set up a similar equation:

$$c \, / \, 2 = v2$$

then

$$v1 - v2 = \text{relative speed between first light signal and second light signal}$$

However, because of special relativity, this can't be so. Think back to Einstein's clocks and measuring rods for reference frames. In order to do this equation as we did in our reality, we have to account for the relativity by the same measures for both of our observers. Each would have to measure space, time, distance, and duration of an event in the exact same way. But if we remember Einstein's clocks, the first astronaut who is still will have a clock moving faster than the second astronaut who is chasing the first light signal. Further, to *all* observers, regardless of other relative elements, the light signal from each vehicle moves (and is perceived to move) identically because the speed of light in unchanging. The speed of light depends on no observer at all.

This revelation of Einstein's is his most important finding to date. In his thought experiment about two astronauts in free space, he concludes:

> For any inertial observer on one of the space stations, every light signal moves through empty space with the same, constant speed: $c = 299,792.458$ kilometers/1 second, independent of the motion of the light source.

He has named our new and only absolute. No longer can we use Newton's mechanics of space and time to understand our place (in motion, or at rest) in the universe.

$E = mc^2$

Special relativity also helps scientists address Newton's idea that the conservation of mass and the conservation of energy are separate entities. To date, it is true, that no object or observer can travel as fast as the speed of light; it is also true that neither can surpass the speed of light. It is believed if we could pass it, we'd be able to time travel.

Because the speed of light is absolute, and thus far in his thought experiments, the other factors of physics (motion/mechanics) are relative, our understanding of mass and energy as separate doesn't hold true to our reality. Since the speed limit of the universe is now the speed of light, all energy and matter must abide this absolute law.

From Newton, we inherit that an object's mass is constant. This is proved in Newton's two separate laws about mass:

$$F = G(m_1 \, m_2) \, / \, r^2$$

which measure's an object's gravitational mass and:

$$F = ma$$

which measure's an object's inertial mass.

In these equations, we get two ways of explaining the same thing: an object's mass. In the second equation, the ratio of force acting on an object changes its acceleration (or deceleration). The mass of the object is determined by its inertial state. This makes seeming sense in our reality. From body weight, to cars, to piles of coal that fill an empty train car, this is a function of our day-to-day reality.

Einstein's special relativity unveils the flaws in this physics, though. In special relativity, the mass of a body is relative to its speed. Quantum physicists at this time are working with machines that can read and measure particles, light waves, etc. It's why the fields of optics and electrodynamics are so crucial to Einstein's work. If we are using a particle accelerator, or working with any kind of radiation or electromagnetic measurements, we are moving particles like atoms, electrons, and photons to speeds near the speed of light. Even in these teeny-tiny bodies, the mass increases as the speed does.

Because the mass increases with speed, we know it's impossible to go the speed of light or to surpass it (at least until other technologies can battle against this seemingly physical truth). Physicists refer to this phenomenon as mass-energy equivalence. Einstein phrases it as:

$$E = mc^2$$

Initially, these findings seem counterintuitive. Classical mechanics gave us the math and ideas, which describe what is visible to us in a given moment. Einstein arrived at a time where the invisible is being made visible. X-rays. Particle accelerators. Televisions. Inventions are bringing us things in life and in space that we didn't know how to see or perceive before. He was able to take listeners and readers into his mind to understand the subtleties in the world at large that we didn't otherwise understand. Ten years after he developed the theory of special relativity, he was able to make broader claims in general relativity, which cosmology continues to find the proofs for today.

The GENERAL THEORY of GENERAL RELATIVITY

One factor special relativity doesn't address is gravity. What role does gravitation play in relativity if at all? Newton had a clear understanding of gravity as being a huge, undeniable force—one that keeps us grounded and keeps the planets in perfect orbit. But as we learn from special relativity, Newton's separate equations for gravitational mass and inertial mass turn out to be measuring the same thing. Einstein found that the effects of gravity (or an object being pulled) are the same as the effects of acceleration (or an object being pushed); this is known as the **principle of equivalence**. Thus, the general theory of relativity will reconcile gravitation in new terms.

Why does Einstein need another theory, though? If we return to our model of the train on the embankment, for example, we have set new physical rules for observed motion. However, we have not accounted for changes in motion. So far, we have a train moving uniformly and an embankment that stays. Einstein now needs to ponder what happens when motion isn't uniform. He also needs to convince us that there is no state of "at rest." Gravitation helps him lay the groundwork for these larger claims. Because we are small, it is hard to imagine experiencing all forms of motion at all times. Einstein explains it to us by returning to the train:

> Let us imagine ourselves transferred to our old friend the railway carriage, which is travelling at a uniform rate. As long as it is moving uniformly, the occupant of the carriage is not sensible of its motion, and it is for this reason that he can un-reluctantly interpret the facts of the case as indicating that the carriage is at rest, but the embankment in motion.

In this case, the special principle of relativity explains the observer's experience. When we ride a train and look out the window, keeping our eyes still, the images reel *past us* as though we were viewing a movie. But, if that uniform motion is interrupted, what are we left with?

> If the motion of the carriage is now changed into a non-uniform motion, as for instance by a powerful application of the brakes, then the occupant of the carriage experiences a correspondingly powerful jerk forwards. The retarded motion is manifested in the mechanical behavior of bodies relative to the person in the railway carriage. The mechanical behavior is different from that of the case previously considered, and for this reason it would appear to be impossible that the same mechanical laws hold relatively to the non-uniformly moving carriage, as

hold with reference to the carriage when at rest or
in uniform motion.

That jolt of the carriage shows us that the reference body of
the train is not the same as the reference body of the observer.
We are left wondering if there can be any physical laws for non-
uniform motion.

Space-Time Continuum

Einstein's former teacher, Hermann Minkowski, understood
Einstein's theory of special relativity. Based on Einstein's work
and the Lorentz transformations, Minkowski offered Einstein
an idea of space-time—a continuum where time and space are
inextricably linked and make up a fourth dimension of how
physics occur in the universe. It is difficult to imagine this.

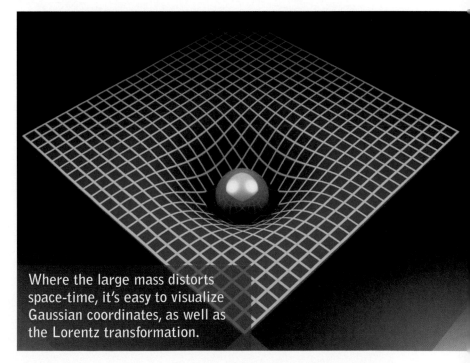

Where the large mass distorts
space-time, it's easy to visualize
Gaussian coordinates, as well as
the Lorentz transformation.

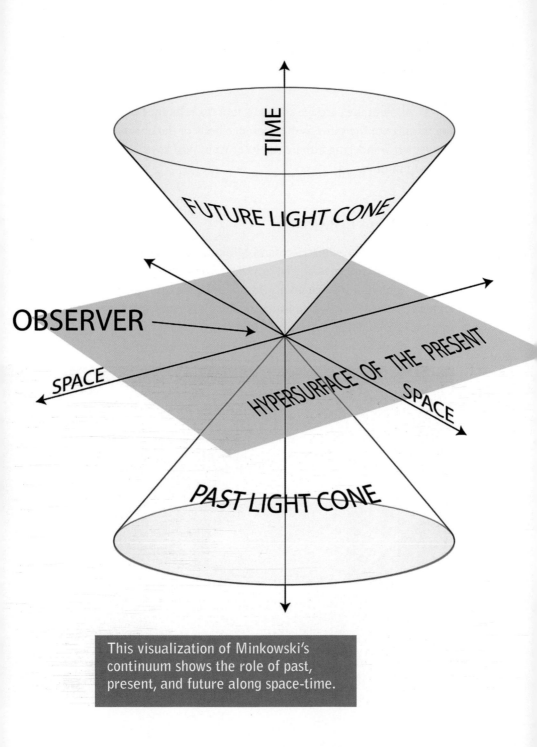

TIME

FUTURE LIGHT CONE

OBSERVER

SPACE

HYPERSURFACE OF THE PRESENT

SPACE

PAST LIGHT CONE

This visualization of Minkowski's continuum shows the role of past, present, and future along space-time.

Einstein understands it as a fabric. Most commonly, we imagine space-time like a trampoline. When nothing is on the trampoline, the fabric is taut. If you placed a bowling ball at the center, the fabric would dip down. If we then took smaller round objects, like marbles, golf balls, and tennis balls, what would happen if we placed them on the fabric?

If we put all three of these near the trampoline's edge and released them, they would all move toward the bowling ball at the center. If we gave them a slight nudge, we would notice that they approach the bowling ball in an orbit. This has more to do with the curve of the fabric (or in the universe, space-time) than with the bowling ball being particularly attractive; they are simply following the curve in space-time. You would also see that the varying masses of each kind of ball would cause them to orbit at different rates.

The Gravitational Field

So, if gravity is part of space-time, how is that different than Newton's gravity? If we look at classical mechanics and special relativity, gravity seems about right with our understanding of it. Bodies in uniform motion move in mostly straight lines like the apple that Newton sees falling from the tree or the stone the observer on the moving train drops down to a footpath. General relativity is concerned with making uniform physical rules for the larger phenomena around it, though. We may think we are at rest, but if we zoom out, Earth is spinning and orbiting the sun, and the sun is spinning and moving toward something greater. And, if we zoom in when we think we are at rest, the same is true. We might be asleep in our bed, but the atoms on our skin are moving, and so are their electrons, and so on.

So if we take this idea of gravity out of 2-D geometry and into space-time, we see some different behaviors than we might expect. Newton's theory of gravity suggests that two objects moving in parallel lines will never converge, unless a force acts upon them. Gravitation is such a force. However, let's say those two objects are moving in the straightest possible lines, but the lines are on a curved surface, like a planet.

In this case, there is no force making the two objects converge. Gravity, in general relativity, is a distortion to space-time. Einstein shows us the difference, first, with our understanding of planets in orbit.

Unlike Kepler's visualization of planet orbits, Einstein suggested that a planet will follow a slight spiral instead of the exact same path.

The Technology Behind Gravitational Lensing

One prediction of general relativity was the existence of binary stars. In the case of these companion stars, either one star revolves around the other, or both revolve around a common center. Gravitational lensing in conjunction with more advanced telescopes and technologies has allowed scientists to observe this behavior.

What's more compelling, still, is that Einstein's relativity and the speed of light predict, rightly, that what we are seeing in the night sky has already happened along space-time. So, then, gravitational lensing can be used to see the same event more than one time (by adding this lens). It can also be used to observe binary or companion stars. In more recent years, the Hubble telescope has captured Sirius—the closest known system of binary stars.

Further, technology in imaging has been able to prove that Einstein's predictions stand even when the stars are dead. The Kepler telescope witnessed a dead star (a white dwarf) crossing in front of a red dwarf in 2013—before this, it was difficult to see because it takes so long for these massive objects to move, and because we don't yet have technologies that can move fast enough and far enough to confirm these events in real time. For example, we don't yet have a satellite that can move back and forth quickly enough to get us this information instantaneously (though, eventually other humans will have this information from the slow-moving things we've sent into space).

According to Newton's theory, a planet moves round the sun in an ellipse, which would permanently maintain its position with respect to the fixed stars, if we could disregard the motion of the fixed stars, themselves and the action of the other planets under consideration. Thus, if we correct the observed motion of the planets for these two influences, and if Newton's theory be strictly correct, we ought to obtain for the orbit of the planet an ellipse, which is fixed with reference to the fixed stars. This deduction, which can be tested with great accuracy, has been confirmed for all the planets save one [...], Mercury.

Kepler's laws of planetary motion, derived from Newton's classical mechanics, predict that Mercury would take an elliptical orbit around the sun.

Einstein's theory predicts a different shape. At the points where Mercury is furthest and closest to the sun, one orbit to the next, those points shift, making a kind of elliptical swirl.

Light and Gravity

Einstein now has to bring light and gravity together. Since gravity is tied to space-time, how does it impact the one absolute, the speed of light? The prediction is clear: gravity will deflect (bend) light. In 1919, the first major proof of Einstein's work would come with a total eclipse.

Einstein predicted that light does not travel in a perfectly straight line. This is because of the curvature of space-time—nothing travels in a straight line because of it. In order to prove this, a group of astronomers realized that astronomical observations would be different during a total eclipse.

When we observe stars in the sky, we consider a star's location. It is more accurate to qualify location as the direction from which the star's light hits us. The astronomers determined that during the total eclipse, the sun would pass a large cluster of stars, the Hyades cluster. The light from those stars would have to pass through the sun's gravitational field. The darkness of the eclipse would allow us to observe the light from this cluster. And so the astronomers set out to measure the shift in the light from these stars.

The near warp did in fact change the observed positions of the stars in the sky. Einstein, who was still obscure in most circles, was in newspapers around the world just after his fortieth birthday.

Today, this phenomenon is called **gravitational lensing**. This discovery and others developed and changed the fields of cosmology and astrophysics drastically. General relativity continues to be proven in new ways all the time as scientists discover more about the universe.

The Hubble Space Telescope captured this image of the barred spiral galaxy in the Ursa Minor constellation.

CHAPTER 5

Influence of the Theory of Relativity

The beautiful thing about many theories in science is that their originators can barely imagine how they will hold up over time. Before he died in 1955, Einstein was able to see some proof of his thought experiments during his lifetime. Since his death, many new ideas and inventions have come into the world, allowing us to continue diving deeply into his theory through experience.

INFLUENCES in COSMOLOGY, ASTROPHYSICS, and ASTRONOMY

The two most immediate examples of Einstein's theory at work were his prediction of Mercury's orbital path around the sun and gravitational lensing (the bending of light waves emitted by stars when passing the sun's gravitational field before hitting Earth during the total eclipse of 1919). As Einstein and others continued coming up with the math that might support relativity, more changes and discoveries came to be. As with these first two examples, the field of cosmology was born, and deeper research was developed in astrophysics and astronomy.

The "Finite" and Yet Unbounded Universe

In his papers on the universal effects of general relativity on the universe, Einstein says that Newton's idea of the universe remains in the finite dimensions of geometry, measured upon 2-D planes. If we are to consider space-time a reality impacted by the matter within it, the universe can't fit into such a finite plane. This relates back to Einstein's understanding of gravity. If straight lines are also inherently curved, because the whole of space-time is curved, then the shape of the universe has to change fundamentally.

Even if humans can experience and articulate things in only two and three dimensions, by placing these articulations on a spherical surface we can realize through Einstein that all attempts at measure will eventually result in a curve. He qualifies this as:

> A self-contained line of definite finite length, which can be measured up by means of a measuring rod; similarly, this universe has a finite area, that can be compared with the area of a square constructed with rods […] *the universe of these beings is finite and yet has no limits.*

This kind of logic has a similar quality to it as our model of multiple sets of infinity, which we looked at closely from a ruler. A standard ruler is a finite 12 inches long. And yet, upon that line, there are an infinite number of points. And between those infinite points, there are another set of infinite points, and so on.

Einstein predicts that even on our finite sphere, we are roaming through something that is expanding. At the time, he and other scientists were unable to confirm this. It wouldn't be until later that we began to see this could be possible, indeed.

Gravitational Waves

One new phenomenon predicted by general relativity is
gravitational waves. Based on Einstein's new qualifications of
gravity and a gravitational field, what (to him) logically follows
are distortions of space-time, which move through its fabric in
the form of waves.

If we think of space-time as fabric, it's not so hard to
imagine that an object in motion would cause a rippling of that
fabric. Einstein's space-time shows us that the origin of gravity
altogether comes from huge objects warping space-time.
Objects like planets, galaxies, supernova, and other bodies and
phenomena can impact the fabric of the universe.

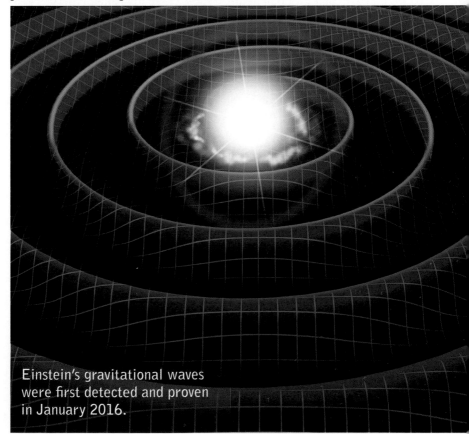

Einstein's gravitational waves
were first detected and proven
in January 2016.

As with relativity, the object distorts based on the direction in which the gravitational wave travels. This also solidifies Einstein's claims about time dilation and **length contraction**. As he says of those phenomena, when mass is accelerated, time and distance change relative to it.

In 2016 the Laser Interferometer Gravitational-Wave Observatory (LIGO) confirmed the existence of gravitational waves. Before this discovery scientists were able to find other phenomena in the universe that implied that his theory was right.

The Max Planck Institute for Gravitational Physics named the primary "smoking gun" for gravitational waves as being one particular group of neutron stars, currently called PSR1913+16. The institute's scientists claim:

> Einstein's theory predicts that gravitational waves carry away energy. For a system of orbiting stars, such a decrease in total energy leads to an ever faster and closer orbit. Over decades, radio astronomers have monitored the time that it takes the stars of PSR1913+16 to complete each successive orbit, and lo and behold: this orbital period decreases over time exactly as predicted by general relativity. This is strong evidence that the speed-up is indeed due to the radiation of gravitational waves, and the reason Russell Hulse and Joseph Taylor were awarded the Nobel Prize for physics for the year 1993.

Similar to the ideas of the big bang theory, what these scientists predicted, ultimately, was a collision either between stars or with a black hole. They knew the energy from a collision this gigantic would result in gravitational waves. Supernovas are another example that implied Einstein's prediction is right. When stars die, they explode, causing huge amounts of energy to be emitted across space-time.

Now that scientists have detected gravitational waves, more ideas associated with them can advance. Like a light wave, sound wave, or water wave, a gravitational wave would carry all kinds of information on it.

First, we can tell where the wave came from. Based on the qualifiers of the wave (frequency, amplification, etc.), we know how much energy produced the wave. A supernova explosion causes a different pulse on space-time than, say, the collision of two black holes.

Thus far, astrophysicists and cosmologists have used radiation to understand faraway objects and phenomena in space. Similar to the X-ray, electromagnetism, and the photons given off by electrons, scientists use radiation to build a picture of origin. Based on a certain reading, an electromagnetic wave can help a scientist understand the size, mass, energy, and other relative factors of a given space object or event, like a galaxy, a star, or a supernova.

According to the Planck Institute, the information from a gravitational wave helps us build a sound rather than an image:

> [Gravitational waves] are similar to a sound waveform that reaches us from an instrument: such a waveform is a harmonic whole, while light would show us all kinds of details about different regions of the instruments ("how the instrument looks"). Just as a sound wave contains information about how the instrument vibrates, the gravitational waves carry information about the events at which they were formed. Most importantly: Almost all astronomical bodies are transparent to gravitational waves. The waves thus carry information that we could not obtain by other means—information about the flow of matter in the heart of a supernova, or about the material properties of merging neutron stars. They

After a star explodes, it leaves a trail of debris.

promise data about regions that would otherwise be hidden, or accessible only indirectly through computer simulations. One such simulation is the density distribution in the center of a supernova, one second after the beginning of the explosion. Brighter regions correspond to higher density.

Though scientists had been eager to observe gravitational waves, their inability to do so until 2016 is good news for us. Such commotion so close to Earth could lead to dire consequences for human life. Luckily, LIGO's technology allowed them to get closer to the action without risk.

Gravitational Redshift

Taking what we know about waves from the Doppler effect and Einstein's ideas about time dilation and length contraction, we can begin to understand another phenomenon: **gravitational redshift**.

Electromagnetic radiation coming off of a mass also moves in a corkscrew.

Recall the Doppler effect: when an ambulance moves toward an observer, it seems the frequency of the siren is higher, while when the ambulance passes the observer, the frequency of the siren seems lower. When an object gives off a light wave instead of a sound wave, a similar effect can happen. When electromagnet radiation from a light wave propagates within a gravitational field, it gets stretched out slightly (as it moves away from the object). Because of the color spectrum of a light, the stretched-out wave reads red to the human eye. This whole phenomena of gravity distorting light as it propagates is gravitational redshifting.

Black Holes

Rethinking a gravitational field still proves one of Einstein's greatest contributions to cosmology and astrophysics. Classical mechanics conceded that gravity was all powerful. But Newton and those who followed his way of thinking had not yet considered gravity's point of origin. For Newton, gravity was one constant force. For Einstein, gravity can be generated in different directions with different strengths in different parts of the universe (along space-time), and therefore, gravity is not a force, but rather, a consequence resulting from warped space-time.

One claim Einstein makes in conjunction with his understanding of mass (that $E = mc^2$) is that the greater an object's mass (or the more *massive* an object is ...), the greater it's gravitational influence will be upon space-time. Following this claim and his broader theory, Einstein eventually works out a handful of equations to accompany the predictions known as the Einstein field equations.

These equations are foundational to the subsequent field of cosmology, which is concerned with the creation of the universe (one theory of which is the big bang theory). The equations explain the metrics of space-time and the gravitational fields that arrive from mass interacting with space-time. One such phenomenon Einstein's work predicts is black holes.

A black hole is an elusive object, full of mystery. The interior of a black hole remains unknown. Based on how other matter reacts to a black hole, we know a little bit about them. A black hole is a region of space-time qualified by the intensity of its gravitational effects. Gravity is so strong in a black hole that no matter can escape its pull. This includes light. In space, black matter and dark matter are two different qualifiers. Black implies that all light is absorbed. Dark implies something unknown. This is useful when thinking of a black hole. It's not empty. It is so massive and powerful that it has absorbed all light that has entered it. A black hole is the ultimate in imagining Einstein's ideas about time dilation and length contraction.

Staring into a black hole, we can see gravitational lensing around the edge.

We know today that black holes are real. Astrophysicists and cosmologists even know some things about how they behave. Einstein, however, was uncertain of his prediction. Though the math suggested it, there was no experiential proof of it during his lifetime. Einstein and other relativists of his time couldn't agree upon whether a black hole would be an actual object, or a phenomenon, or nonexistent.

Black holes aren't solid. They occupy a region of space-time. When a large star dies, it eventually explodes. This leads to a collapse. Unlike a collapse on Earth, there is no ground to stop the matter that is collapsing. And in the case of massive stars, the collapse is so large that the radius of it turns into a black hole.

Nothing can escape a black hole. And we cannot see what is inside it (at least not yet). The other peculiar thing about black holes, as hypothesized by contemporary physicist Roger Penrose, is that the space-time outside of the black hole's radius behaves as it would have before. A black hole is like the Bermuda triangle in that way. Penrose claims that the black hole is confined to its event horizon.

If we think back to Einstein breaking down absolute time and absolute space, we can recall the importance of the word "event." In 4-D space-time, the coordinates of an event can be placed in space-time. It's as though a black hole exists in the moment of its collapse, permanently.

A Deeper Look at Gravitational Lensing

After the total eclipse of 1919, proof of gravitational lensing led astrophysicists and astronomers to continue conducting measures of the phenomenon. Especially as we discover more astronomical objects, scientists can use this phenomenon to judge the mass (how *massive*) a given object in space is. If light bends that drastically in our own universe near the gravitational field of the sun, then it must bend even more when entering larger gravitational fields.

One such example is a black hole. Now that we have proof of black holes, astronomers want to know more about them—about how they behave and how other matter behaves with them. Gravitational lensing allows astronomers to chart and judge what is behind a black hole (or any other massive object). The bent light is a lens for where the light originated from.

Beyond a total eclipse, what could this phenomenon show us? If we think about objects far more massive than the ones near us—things like black holes, neutron stars, pulsars, etc.—and we think of greater distances, the opportunities for seeing things are vast.

Just two years ago, NASA's Kepler telescope helped scientists reaffirm Einstein's relativity with a new discovery: a white dwarf bending the light of its companion star.

Another amazing use of gravitational lensing is to see events more than once. Recently, scientists were able to use the Hubble telescope to see a supernova more than eight billion light-years away. Because the supernova occurred behind a galaxy, the gravity of that galaxy bent the light of the supernova, allowing scientists to observe it four times. Because it took the light of the supernova time to reach the gravitational field of the galaxy, and then more time to reach Earth, the signaling of each wave (like the Doppler effect) reached us at different times.

Like many other phenomena predicted by relativity, more discoveries continue to prove Einstein right.

The Big Bang Theory

Einstein's understanding of gravity and the general theory of relativity resulted in Einstein's field equations. Unlike Newton's absolute rules for the universe as we experience it, Einstein's theories determined that the universe was constantly changing. He needed new equations to account for this belief of how the universe works. These ten equations became the foundation for the field of cosmology.

Cosmologists are focused on how the universe began. By answering Einstein's field equations, they can understand the shape of the universe (and within it, space-time). These metrics can allow them to understand the history of phenomena in space—of what happened light-years ago, and how.

Because of the solutions these cosmologists found, the big bang theory arose. As predicted by Einstein's work, the big bang theory says that the universe is expanding, that it began expanding from a collision of extremely dense matter at a very high heat.

From the 1920s until now, this theory has paved the way for cosmologists like Edwin Hubble, Roger Penrose, and Stephen Hawking to learn more about the shape of the universe and what it says about the past and the future.

INFLUENCES in OUR EVERYDAY LIFE

Even in the hundred years since Einstein proposed his theories of special and general relativity, technological advances have proven him right time and again and have shown us more about the universe than Einstein could have ever imagined knowing.

GPS

Global Positioning System, or GPS, is probably our most common day-to-day encounter with relativity. These days, it's so common that most of us have it in our smartphones, cars, laptops, and the like. And when we aren't being tracked, but we need to do some tracking, a simple search on Google Maps can show us what we need in an instant.

Your GPS device needs to connect to a satellite to figure out your location. In order to get pinpoint accuracy, it needs relative factors to calculate and recalculate your motion and location. One such factor is time dilation. A satellite orbits Earth at a high speed—not as fast as the speed of light, but still, faster than we can imagine going. This high rate of energy causes the satellite to experience time dilation. In this case, the satellite experiences time more quickly than we do.

And so, your GPS accounts for this by using clocks that account for the difference of these microseconds—it measures our time relative to the satellites. The satellites and GPS software also account for the effects of gravity. Otherwise, our GPS would be off by our location for any number of miles of traveling distance.

Electromagnets

If we think back to Einstein's early thought experiments, we can recall his sixteen-year-old self at school contemplating chasing a light beam and magnet and conductor for the first time. Electrodynamics and optics are very relevant to his early thinking. The mysteries of how particles and waves (or currents) behave help him find flaws in classical mechanics.

An electromagnet is a magnet with a wire coiled around it; its magnetic field is made by electric currents. Science writer Caroline Reid describes the role of relativity in an electromagnet as follows:

> Only some metals are naturally magnetic, like iron, for example. That being said, it is possible to create a magnet out of any metal by turning it into a coil of wire and running an electric current through it. These electrified metals have a strange property: they only magnetically affect objects that are moving and they don't have any effect on stationary objects. This is an electromagnet, and it is thanks to special relativity that this phenomenon is possible.

Electric current is the flow of free-moving electrons through a metal, surrounded by a grid of stationary protons. If a charged object sits still next to an electromagnet, then nothing happens to it. Even though the electrons are flowing, they occupy a similar amount of space to the protons so that over all the electrified metal has no effect on it.

However, if this charged object moves alongside the wire, then it starts to feel the effects of length contraction in the moving electrons. This means that the density of stationary protons becomes larger than the flowing electrons and the metal exhibits a positive charge, causing the object to be attracted or repelled.

Today, electromagnets are used in all kinds of mechanical objects. Some we use every day are speakers and motors. Many factory machines use electromagnets as well, especially places like scrap yards, in which heavy, magnetic objects need to be moved.

One of the more urgent uses of electromagnets is in medical machinery. MRI and X-ray readings, for example, use electromagnetic radiation to gather images from inside the body. In order to capture these images, electromagnets are used in the machines.

Television

It's hard to imagine this now, but televisions used to look very different. They were big clunky cubes. The screens were rounded like a lens. They had knobs and dials on them. And they had antennae sticking out of them. TVs and their monitors used cathode ray tubes to fire electrons between the TV screen and a magnet.

These electrons moved very quickly. Because of this quickened speed, relativity was used to counter length contraction. If we think of TV or video game images looking "wonky," we can imagine that inside, the cathode ray tube and magnet could need a little tap or shake to return to relative states of length contraction.

Gold's Color

The decade following Einstein's first presentation of relativity in 1905, he was developing general relativity. And during that same decade, because of his findings, Niels Bohr suggested his new model of the atom. The key relativistic factor of this atom was the behavior of electrons: they could jump between orbitals, and in doing so, they emitted photons of light.

The color of gold isn't arbitrary or naturally given. Actually, based on gold's atomic makeup, it should give off a more silver sheen. Rather, gold's color occurs as a consequence of relativity and the atomic level. This strange mystery can be explained when looking at the atom a little more closely. Science writer Caroline Reid describes the process as follows:

> There is a total of 79 electrons zooming around a gold atom, and 79 protons in the nucleus. In the orbital closest to the nucleus (otherwise known as the 1s orbital), the electrons have to move at a shockingly fast speed. They move at roughly ½ the speed of light to avoid being dragged into the nucleus by the powerful positive charge from the protons in the nucleus, and that causes a lot of relativistic effects.
>
> Because the electrons are moving so fast, the separate electron shells appear to be closer than they actually are. For an electron to jump to a higher energy level it needs to absorb a specific wavelength of light.

In gold, the wavelengths that could be absorbed are usually in the ultraviolet range—beyond what we can see. However, when we account for the relativistic effects that appear to squeeze the shells closer together, we find that the gold actually starts to absorb light with a smaller frequency: blue light.

The blue light is absorbed and only the red colors are reflected into our eyes. Hence, gold has a glamorous, yellowy sheen.

These relative atomic factors also make it difficult for gold to corrode. It's why we value this precious metal so greatly. Because gold is so dense, the electrons are heavier than usual and hover closely to the atom's nucleus. Also, let's not forget about Einstein's $E = mc^2$. It functions at the subatomic level, too. So when a heavy electron (high mass) jumps orbits, the photon produced has a higher energy than usual. A gold atom is a tiny model of the universe at large and functions with the same rules as the cosmos, just as Einstein predicted.

Nuclear Plants

Einstein's principle of equivalence in relativity is why energy and mass are (relatively) the same. Nuclear power plants function on this idea. They use a nuclear reactor to generate heat. The steam emitted rotates a steam turbine. The steam turbine is connected to an electric generator that uses the turbine's thermal energy to make electricity.

Thermometers

Because of relativity, our encounters with mercury are in a liquid state. Like gold, mercury is a very heavy atom.

The makeup of its heavy electrons has a similar effect as gold's—the atoms are close to the nucleus and the mass of those electrons increases when jumping orbits. Mercury's atomic makeup and chemical nature make it melt at lower temperatures than other matter.

The inverse is also true. One of the best-known uses of liquid mercury is the glass thermometer. A physicist named Daniel Gabriel Fahrenheit invented it in the early 1700s. Because of relativity, the volume of mercury changes with temperature, which is why a higher temperature causes the volume of mercury to rise in the glass tube. Today, many of us use digital thermometers, but the glass thermometer will never be inaccurate due to a dying battery.

SCOTT KELLY and TIME TRAVEL

One idea we know about time travel is that if we go up into space, time will pass more rapidly, and thus, when we land back on Earth, we will have aged more quickly than we would have on Earth. This idea was first thought of by Einstein. As of spring 2016, the results of this idea are being put to the test. Astronaut Scott Kelly spent one year in space. Since his return, NASA has been figuring out the effects of his quickened aging. Scientists had predicted that despite certain aging effects, other specific symptoms of aging and degeneration might lessen due to other factors in space. Kelly's DNA is being compared to that of his twin brother to help make all kinds of assessments.

CONCLUSIONS: SPECIAL and GENERAL

It is hard to unsee the tremendous influence of Einstein's work on the universe—be that the atomic universe or the universe at large. Every decade, more findings prove to us the merits of his gedankenexperiments, starting from the time he was just a teenager.

The stunning thing about a theory is that it can signal previous knowledge and call forth experiences of the present and future all at once. Einstein could not have imagined the consequences and discoveries that sprang from his ideas. He was able to see many significant turning points during his lifetime—the full eclipse, the race to nuclear weapons, and the like. But the truth about black holes, gravitational waves, and other galactic phenomena are things that are new to our understanding of the universe. And more is out there to be discovered—things we won't be able to see either. It's the legacy of this theory that is a rare world gift. And it was born out of such attention to beauty and urgency.

Like many scientists of modern times, it's also difficult to unsee this urgency. The number of Jewish scientists with Nobel Prizes from this time alone is a testament to the power of urgency. Simultaneous to trying to make the atomic bomb, Alan Turing was inventing a machine to beat the Germans—a machine we know today as a computer. We are just beginning to put back together the fabric of details from that trying time in human history—from the discoveries, to the predicaments that instigated such changes. As our world continues to become violent once again, we can wonder what discoveries urgency can lead us to—what inventions, great and harmful, may befall again as another century has turned.

Perhaps the greatest lesson of Einstein's is one in imagination. Without it, Einstein would not have been able to see and foresee these scientific truths. When we think of daydreamers, we often think of artists. Einstein was that, too—a philosopher and writer as much as he was anything else. Because of his "radical" ways of being in the world, of imagining it first and measuring it second, he was able to transcend many fields of thinking, seeing, and even believing. In his later life, he often spoke of the need for imagination. Most famously, perhaps is this from an interview with the *Post* in 1929:

> I am enough of an artist to draw freely upon my imagination. Imagination is more important than knowledge. For knowledge is limited to all we know and understand, while imagination embraces the entire world, and all there will ever be to know and understand.

Careful reasoning. Measuring. Calculating. These are the skills that we often measure in schools and in work. But, to paraphrase Oskar Schindler, if we added even just a bit of imagination to that, we might just be able to see and save the world entire.

Physics or Politics?
The Atomic Bomb

Though there were some initial criticisms of Einstein's theories, none stand today. His work continues to be proven by scientists (as well as humanities scholars) across many fields of study every day. From 1905 to 1919, the world went from simply pondering what the ideas of this young, obscure man meant, to knowing that what we inherited from Newton was imprecise at best, and that Einstein was giving us the universe closer to its true form.

One criticism or question that arises from the twentieth century at large is how to feel about the atomic bomb. Nuclear weapons, in general, have large political camps on every side of the spectrum, especially in today's world where terrorism is on the rise. Though it's not a criticism of Einstein's work, the idea of building an atomic bomb was first his.

In 1939, comrades of Einstein's, Leo Szilard and Eugene Wigner, drafted a letter to US president Franklin Delano Roosevelt. The contents of the letter explained to the president the possibility of Germany developing an atomic bomb. Szilard was the physicist who imagined and invented the first nuclear chain reaction. Szilard dictated the letter in German, Wigner wrote it down, and Einstein signed it. Roosevelt's response to the letter was the Manhattan Project.

The Manhattan Project was a group of some of the world's most powerful scientists in conjunction with the US military researching and developing the first atomic bomb.

As the West continues to be criticized in an ever-changing world, it's hard to ignore the moment in history of this weapon as one of the central events for which we will be judged throughout time. On the other hand, these physicists were on the brink of thrilling science.

In the specific case of Einstein—a German Jew who escaped to America during the war while his books were being burned across his homeland—the urgency with which he signed that letter is not only serious, but relative to the events of his life's predicaments.

Nuclear fission, which led to the success of the atomic bomb, uses relativity as a key ingredient. $E=mc^2$ allowed physicists to understand the nuclei of particular atoms very deeply and precisely. Eventually, the Manhattan Project built an atomic bomb before the Nazis and before anyone else.

Chronology

1687 Isaac Newton's *Philosophiae Naturalis Principia Mathematica* is published

1738 David Hume's "A Treatise of Human Nature" is published and states that time is not a separate entity from the objects/observers that experience it

1758 Newton's laws of motion and universal gravity are proven true when a comet returns to the visible night sky; we know the comet today as Halley's comet, named for Edmond Halley, the astronomer who had seen it and tracked it in instances prior

1801 Thomas Young performs the first version of the double-slit experiment

1842 The Doppler effect is presented by Christian Doppler

1865 James Clerk Maxwell publishes *A Dynamical Theory of the Electromagnetic Field*

1879 Albert Einstein is born in Germany; James Clerk Maxwell dies

1895 German physicist Wilhelm Röntgen discovers X-rays

1896 According to Einstein's *Autobiographical Notes*, "Chasing a Beam of Light" occurs when he's sixteen years old, in which he realizes that the presence of any observer chasing after a light beam will only be adequate to see a frozen light wave

1905 Einstein's publications come together as the theory of special relativity; Einstein solves the paradox of the photoelectric effect

1915 Einstein publishes the theory of general relativity

1917 Einstein applies general relativity to a model of the universe, advancing cosmology by adding a "cosmological constant" to account for gravity

1919 Einstein's theory gets its first major proof during a total eclipse when gravity bends light in the way he predicted

1920 Einstein first visits America

1922 Einstein wins the Nobel Prize

1925 Einstein and Niels Bohr have a series of public debates about quantum mechanics; Einstein is the figurehead for newly opened Hebrew University of Jerusalem

1929 Edwin Hubble finds redshift—evidence the universe is expanding—in conjunction with Einstein's equations

1933 Einstein becomes a refugee and immigrates to the US to escape the Nazi regime; he saves one thousand German-Jewish scientists by convincing Turkey to take them in as refugees

1938 Nuclear fission is first discovered in Berlin by Otto Hahn, Lise Meitner, and Fritz Strassmann

1939 Einstein, Szilárd, and Wigner write to Roosevelt encouraging him to build nuclear weapons before the Nazis do

1940 Einstein becomes a US citizen

1942 The Manhattan Project begins in pursuit of creating the first atomic bomb

1945 The Manhattan Project tests the first atomic bomb; a month later, the US drops two atomic bombs on Japan

1955 Einstein dies of an aneurism

1959 Redshift is observed by Harvard physicists

1964 First experimental evidence of the big bang

1968 Relativistic delay of light observed

1970 Stephen Hawking postulates that black holes emit radiation by using relativity and quantum theory

1974 Stephen Hawking proves that black holes aren't vacuums, known as Hawking radiation

1976 Gravity Probe A confirms time ticks faster in space than on Earth

1988 Stephen Hawking publishes *A Brief History of Time: From the Big Bang to Black Holes*

1998 Dark energy is discovered, proving the accelerated expansion of the universe

2002 Stephen Hawking publishes *The Theory of Everything: The Origin and Fate of the Universe*

2002 Direct detection of gravitational waves by LIGO

2004 Gravity Probe B observes Earth's disruption of space-time

2016 French mission MICROSCOPE will measure free fall in space

absolute space Newton's idea of space as unable to be impacted by physical events.

absolute time Newton's idea that time is constant and free of being impacted.

astronomy The study of celestial objects.

astrophysics A branch of science in which the laws of physics and chemistry are used to explain phenomena in the universe at large.

atomic physics The study of atoms as isolated pieces of matter and the subatomic matter contained therein.

classical mechanics The study of motion; also referred to as Newtonian physics.

cosmology The science of the creation and development of the universe.

Doppler effect An increase or decrease in the frequency of a propagated wave (light, sound, etc.) as the source of the propagated wave and the observer of the wave move closer or farther from each other. The effect (of changed frequency) causes sudden changes in the perception of the propagated wave (for example, the pitch of a siren or in space, the perceived color of a star based on whether it is moving toward or away from Earth).

double-slit experiment An experiment in which matter or waves are shot at a blank wall, and a wall with two slits is placed in the middle of the trajectory. If the matter being shot at the blank wall is a wave, a lattice pattern and/or spectrum will appear on the blank wall; if, on the other hand, particles are shot at the blank wall, there will be two lines or beams parallel to the double slits that the particles travel through to hit the blank wall. Photons of light behave as a wave when no observer is present but as a particle when a camera (observer) is placed to observe the photon traveling through the experiment.

$E = mc^2$ Einstein's famous equation, suggesting that energy and mass are equivalent, and that the speed of light is constant (does not regard other factors to be determined).

electrodynamics A field within mechanics steeped in the impacts and effects of electric and magnetic fields; the kinetics of electric currents.

Galilean transformation An understanding of movement between two coordinates on a given plane as described by the rules of Newton and classical mechanics; understanding the movement between coordinates in two or three dimensions.

gedankenexperiment "Thought experiment"; Einstein's word for his conceptual imaginings as origin of the mathematical and experiential proofing to come later.

general relativity A theory proposing that the motion of objects, whether massive or minute (cosmic, or subatomic), is relative to other factors on the space-time continuum, especially, a given gravitational field that disrupts space-time.

gravitational field The field of gravity around a massive object caused by its energy, producing a force field in its vicinity along space-time.

gravitational lensing Energy density curves space-time, resulting in the deflection of a light ray; gravity bends light.

gravitational mass Newton's equation that articulates a moving object's ability to stop; $F = G(m_1\, m_2)\,/\,r^2$ in which something lands in a gravitational field.

gravitational redshift Explanation for the change (reduction) in frequency of electromagnetic radiation when observed from a weaker gravitational field than the one in which the electromagnetic radiation originated.

gravitational waves Einstein's theory of general relativity suggests that large gravitational fields cause waves along the space-time continuum; gravitational waves have not yet been proven directly, though most physicists believe they exist based on other phenomena of cosmology.

inertial mass Newton's equation $F=ma$ for how much force is needed to get something moving.

inertial observer An observer who is at rest. Newton qualifies this as an observer not in motion. Einstein later elaborates that the state of "at rest" can only exist outside of a gravitational field, and thus, an inertial observer is an observer in an inertial reference-frame (a gravity-free space).

in vacuo The Latin term for "in a vacuum," used by scientists to describe tests with controlled environments.

length contraction An object at rest will hold a different measurement of length then when it's in motion as measured by a stationary observer; an object's contraction will increase as its speed does. See also *time dilation*.

Lorentz transformation Marking the movement between coordinates relative to their constant states of motion or constant states of rest. Unlike the Galilean transformations, Lorentz transformations can include the rotation of space, the understanding of multiple reference bodies, and space-time.

multiple sets of infinity A phenomena in which different measures of infinity can be larger or smaller than one another.

principle of equivalence The effects of gravity and the effects of acceleration are equivalent; $E = mc^2$; mass-energy equivalence.

quantum mechanics The scientific principles that explain how matter behaves—be it cosmic matter, atomic matter, or any other matter; the specific math and quanta that explain the behavior of matter.

redshift When light or electromagnetic radiation coming from an object occurs at a high frequency and reads red, or the highest on the spectrum of such a wave.

reference body A system of coordinates for a given object or body. This qualifier allowed Einstein to separate phenomena in special and general relativity. In his thought experiment proving special relativity, the coordinates by which we mark time on a moving train are specific and separate than that of the embankment along which the train moves. Farther out, the reference body for the planet is separate than those smaller instances of motion. This is the precursor for proving space-time. See also *Galilean transformations* and *Lorentz transformations*.

relativity of simultaneity Einstein's idea, based on special and general relativity, that simultaneity depends on an observer's frame of reference.

space-time A woven continuum of space and time; 4-D space and time.

special relativity Einstein's idea that, unlike prior understandings of physics, certain perceptions about space and time are relative to one another, and not absolute.

time dilation The phenomena of two different times occurring due to the relativistic nature of time and space; an object in motion experiences slower time than an object at rest (or relatively at rest). See also *length contraction*.

universal gravitation Newton's law of attraction, stating that all objects attract each other with a force of gravitational attraction. Einstein proves this to be untrue as the origin of gravity is not universal, but rather, relative to a given massive body's ability to disrupt space-time, causing other reactions (such as particular planets in orbit relative to our particular sun). The equation used by Newton to prove this originally was $F = G(m_1 \, m_2) \, / \, r^2$.

Further Information

BOOKS

Calaprice, Alice, Daniel Kennefick, and Robert Schulmann. *An Einstein Encyclopedia*. Princeton, NJ: Princeton University Press, 2015.

Halpern, Paul. *Einstein's Dice and Schrödinger's Cat: How Two Great Minds Battled Quantum Randomness to Create a Unified Theory of Physics*. New York, NY: Basic Books, 2015.

Kaku, Michio. *Einstein's Cosmos: How Albert Einstein's Vision Transformed Our Understanding of Space and Time*. New York, NY: W.W. Norton & Company, 2004.

WEBSITES

Albert Einstein Institution
http://www.aeinstein.org

The mission of this nonprofit organization is to advance the study and use of strategic nonviolent action in conflicts throughout the world. The organization uses Einstein's model of resistance to war, as well as rethinking how to support war against the Nazi regime, to help conflicts. This is a great tool to learn about how science can't be apolitical, the role of translation in granting democratic access to information, and how to think about science and cultural urgency.

Einstein Archives Online
http://www.alberteinstein.info

This site is a database of Einstein's papers, a timeline of his work, and a gallery with images of his papers and from his personal life. The archives are a joint project of the Albert Einstein Archives of the Hebrew University of Jerusalem with the support of the Polonsky Foundation, and the Einstein Papers Project at California Institute of Technology with the support of Princeton University Press.

Einstein Online
http://www.einstein-online.info

Provided by the Max Planck Institute for Gravitational Studies, Einstein Online breaks down Einstein's theories of relativity for beginners who want to learn more about the math, science, and modern-day applications of Einstein's work.

FILMS

Einstein and Eddington. Directed by Philip Martin. Performed by David Tennant, Andy Serkis. USA: HBO Films, 2008.

Einstein Revealed. Directed by Peter Jones. Performed by Andrew Sachs. USA: WGBH, 1996.

Einstein's Big Idea. Directed by Gary Johnstone. USA: WGBH Boston Video, 2005.

Bibliography

Australia Telescope National Facility. "Galileo and Newton." Accessed November 23, 2015 (http://www.atnf.csiro.au/outreach/education/senior/cosmicengine/galileo_newton.html).

Bohr, Niels. "Discussions with Einstein on Epistemological Problems in Atomic Physics." Cambridge University Press, 1949. Accessed November 26, 2015 (https://www.marxists.org/reference/subject/philosophy/works/dk/bohr.htm).

Born, Max. *Einstein's Theory of Relativity*. New York, NY: Dover Publications, 1962.

Buchen, Lizzie. "May 29, 1919: A Major Eclipse, Relatively Speaking." Wired.com, May 29, 2009. Accessed November 22, 2015 (http://www.wired.com/2009/05/dayintech_0529).

Clavin, Whitney. "Gravity-Bending Find Leads to Kepler Meeting Einstein." NASA/JPL, April 4, 2013. Accessed November 22, 2015 (http://www.jpl.nasa.gov/news/news.php?release=2013-124).

Einstein, Albert. *Relativity: The Special and the General Theory*. Translated by Robert W. Lawson. Mockingbird Classics Publishing, 2015.

Emspak, Jesse. "8 Ways You Can See Einstein's Theory of Relativity in Real Life." LiveScience, November 26, 2014. Accessed November 22, 2015 (http://www.livescience.com/48922-theory-of-relativity-in-real-life.html).

"How Einstein's Theory of Relativity Changed the World." YouTube. November 25, 2015 (Accessed March 01, 2016. https://www.youtube.com/watch?v=9hExd7u4lxE).

Isaacson, Walter. *Einstein: His Life and Universe*. New York, NY: Simon & Schuster Paperbacks, 2007.

Kaiser, David. "How Politics Shaped General Relativity." *New York Times*. November 06, 2015. Accessed March 01, 2016 (http://www.nytimes.com/2015/11/08/opinion/how-politics-shaped-general-relativity.html?_r=0).

Kaiser, David. "Who Did What When? A Time Line of $E = mc^2$." PBS. Accessed March 01, 2016 (http://www.pbs.org/wgbh/nova/education/activities/3213_einstein_06.html).

"Letter from Albert Einstein to FDR." PBS. Accessed March 01, 2016 (http://www.pbs.org/wgbh/americanexperience/features/primary-resources/truman-ein39/).

Limer, Eric. "Everything You Should Know About Einstein's Theory of General Relativity in Under Three Minutes." *Popular Mechanics*, November 4, 2015. Accessed November 4, 2015. (http://www.popularmechanics.com/science/a18072/general-relativity-primer-under-three-minutes).

Norton, John D. "Einstein's Pathway to Special Relativity." Accessed November 23, 2015. (http://www.pitt.edu/~jdnorton/teaching/HPS_0410/chapters_2015_Jan_1/origins_pathway/index.html).

Overbye, Dennis. "A Century Ago, Einstein's Theory of Relativity Changed Everything." *New York Times*. November 24, 2015. Accessed March 01, 2016 (http://www.nytimes.com/2015/11/24/science/a-century-ago-einsteins-theory-of-relativity-changed-everything.html).

Pais, Abraham. *Subtle Is the Lord: The Science and the Life of Albert Einstein*. Oxford, England: Oxford University Press, 1982.

Redd, Nola Taylor. "Einstein's Theory of General Relativity: A Simplified Explanation | Space.com." Space and NASA News, April 10, 2015. Accessed November 6, 2015. (http://www.space.com/17661-theory-general-relativity.html).

Reid, Caroline. "4 Ways You Can Observe Relativity in Everyday Life." IFLScience, October 7, 2015. Accessed November 22, 2015 (http://www.iflscience.com/physics/4-examples-relativity-everyday-life).

Roston, Michael. "Albert Einstein and Relativity in the Pages of *The Times.*" *New York Times.* November 24, 2015. Accessed March 01, 2016 (http://www.nytimes.com/interactive/2015/11/23/science/albert-einstein-general-relativity.html?_r=1).

"Special Relativity." Einstein Online. Accessed March 1, 2016 (http://www.einstein-online.info/elementary/specialRT).

Wintle, Justin. *Makers of Nineteenth Century Culture: 1800-1914.* London: Routledge & Kegan Paul, 1982.

About the Author

LISA HITON is a filmmaker and poet from Deerfield, Illinois. She went to film school at Boston University, where she fell in love with the practical physics of lighting, composition, and sound. Her love of physics extends into quantum theory. She teaches poetry, film, and literature at many universities on the East Coast. She also holds an MFA in poetry from Boston University and an MEd in arts in education from Harvard University.